What People Are
Threshold Bik

"Stephen Binz's Threshold Bible Study is a marvelous project. With lucidity and creativity, Binz offers today's believing communities a rich and accessible treasury of biblical scholarship. The series' brilliance lies in its simplicity of presentation complemented by critical depth of thought and reflective insight. This is a wonderful gift for personal and communal study, especially for those wishing to make a home for the Word in their hearts."
Carol J. Dempsey, OP, Associate Professor of Theology, University of Portland, OR

"Threshold Bible Study accurately describes this user-friendly series that is aimed at anyone interested in a serious study of the Bible, whether alone or in a group. Written in a sprightly easy-to-understand style, these volumes will engage the mind, heart, and spirit of the reader who utilizes the helpful resources author Stephen J. Binz makes available."
Alexander A. Di Lella, OFM, Andrews-Kelly-Ryan Professor of Biblical Studies, The Catholic University of America

"God's Holy Word addresses the deepest levels of our lives with the assurance of divine grace and wisdom for our individual and communal faith. I am grateful for this new series introducing our Catholic people to the riches of Sacred Scripture. May these guides to understanding the great truths of our redemption bring us all closer to the Lord of our salvation."
Most Reverend Timothy M. Dolan, Archbishop of New York

"Threshold Bible Study offers solid scholarship and spiritual depth. Drawing on the Church's living tradition and the Jewish roots of the New Testament, Threshold Bible Study can be counted on for lively individual study and prayer, even while it offers spiritual riches to deepen communal conversation and reflection among the people of God."
Scott Hahn, Professor of biblical theology, Franciscan University of Steubenville

"Threshold Bible Study offers those who want to begin faith-filled and prayerful study of the Bible a user-friendly tool that is made just for them. Each volume is made up of short chapters with a biblical text, a brief but insightful commentary, focused questions, and a prayer. These books will open readers to a new and stimulating way to encounter the Word of God."
Leslie J. Hoppe, OFM, Professor of Old Testament Studies, Catholic Theological Union, Chicago

"I most strongly recommend Stephen Binz's Threshold Bible Study for adult Bible classes, religious education, and personal spiritual enrichment. The series is exceptional for its scholarly solidity, pastoral practicality, and clarity of presentation. The Church owes Binz a great debt of gratitude for his generous and competent labor in the service of the Word of God."
Peter C. Phan, The Ignacio Ellacuria Professor of Catholic Social Thought, Georgetown University

"Stephen Binz has an amazing gift for making the meaning of the biblical text come alive! With a strong background in Bible study, he knows how to provide the road map any group can use to explore Scripture. Using the method known as *lectio divina*, Threshold Bible Study provides two things: growth in understanding the sacred text, and at the same time, the opportunity for actual conversion as the text is broken open and shared. I'd like to put this into the hands of every adult Catholic in the Church today."

Bill Huebsch, author and theologian, Director of PastoralPlanning.com

"Threshold Bible Study is a refreshing approach to enable participants to ponder the Scriptures more deeply. The thematic material is clearly presented with a mix of information and spiritual nourishment. The questions are thoughtful and the principles for group discussion are quite helpful. This series provides a practical way for faithful people to get to know the Bible better and to enjoy the fruits of biblical prayer."

Irene Nowell, OSB, Mount St. Scholastica, Atchison, Kansas,
Editorial committee for Old Testament translation of the *New American Bible*

"Threshold Bible Study is appropriately named, for its commentary and study questions bring people to the threshold of the text and invite them in. The questions guide but do not dominate. They lead readers to ponder and wrestle with the biblical passages and take them across the threshold toward life with God. Stephen Binz's work stands in the tradition of the biblical renewal movement and brings it back to life. We need more of this in the Church."

Kathleen M. O'Connor, Professor of Old Testament,
Columbia Theological Seminary

"Threshold Bible Study is the perfect series of Bible study books for serious students with limited time. Each lesson is brief, illuminating, challenging, wittily written, and a pleasure to study. The reader will reap a rich harvest of wisdom from the efforts expended."

John J. Pilch, Adjunct Professor of Biblical Studies,
Georgetown University, Washington, DC

"Stephen Binz has put together a great aid in one of the most important aspects of Catholic Christian life today: Bible study. Largely the purview for non-Catholic Christian laity in the past, recent years have seen Catholic hungering for Scripture study and application in their daily lives. Stephen Binz's series promises to help meet that need."

John Michael Talbot, Catholic Christian Recording Artist,
Founder of The Brothers and Sisters of Charity at Little Portion Hermitage

"Threshold Bible Study unlocks the Scriptures and ushers the reader over the threshold into the world of God's living Word. The world of the Bible comes alive with new meaning and understanding for our times. This series enables the reader to appreciate contemporary biblical scholarship and the meaning of God's Word. This is the best material I have seen for serious Bible study."

Most Reverend Donald W. Trautman, Bishop of Erie

THRESHOLD
BIBLE STUDY

JESUS,
the MESSIANIC
KING

PART ONE

Matthew
[1–16]

STEPHEN J. BINZ

TWENTY-THIRD
PUBLICATIONS
twentythirdpublications.com

Third Printing 2016

TWENTY-THIRD PUBLICATIONS
A Division of Bayard
One Montauk Avenue, Suite 200
New London, CT 06320
(860)437-3012 or (800) 321-0411
www.twentythirdpublications.com

ISBN 978-1-58595-815-3
Library of Congress Control Number: 2010938680
Printed in the U.S.A.

 A division of Bayard, Inc.

Contents

HOW TO USE THRESHOLD BIBLE STUDY   v

Suggestions for Individual Study   vii

Suggestions for Group Study   viii

INTRODUCTION   1

Suggestions for Facilitators, Group Session 1   9

LESSONS 1–6

1. Descendant of Abraham and David (Matthew 1:1–17)   10
2. The Messiah's Royal Birth (Matthew 1:18–25)   14
3. Homage and Gifts for the King (Matthew 2:1–12)   17
4. Escape to Egypt and Return to Israel (Matthew 2:13–23)   21
5. God's Kingdom Is at Hand (Matthew 3:1–17)   25
6. Messianic Temptations and the Call of Disciples
   (Matthew 4:1–25)   29

Suggestions for Facilitators, Group Session 2   33

LESSONS 7–12

7. Discourse on the Mountain (Matthew 5:1–16)   34
8. Ethics of the Kingdom (Matthew 5:17–37)   38
9. The Principle of Radical Love (Matthew 5:38–48)   42
10. Spiritual Practices within the Kingdom (Matthew 6:1–23)   46
11. Wealth, Anxiety, and Trust (Matthew 6:24–34)   50
12. Wisdom under God's Reign (Matthew 7:1–28)   54

Suggestions for Facilitators, Group Session 3   58

LESSONS 13–18

13. The Messiah's Healing Work (Matthew 8:1–17)   59
14. The Messiah Manifests Divine Power (Matthew 8:18—9:8)   63
15. New Discipleship for a New Age (Matthew 9:9–17)   67
16. A Ministry of Compassion (Matthew 9:18–34)   71
17. Sharing the Mission of Jesus (Matthew 9:35—10:23)   74
18. Facing the Costs of Discipleship (Matthew 10:24–39)   79
Suggestions for Facilitators, Group Session 4   82

LESSONS 19–24

19. The Messenger Who Prepared the Way (Matthew 11:1–15)   83
20. Jesus Responds to Rejection (Matthew 11:16–30)   87
21. God's Servant Is Lord of the Sabbath (Matthew 12:1–21)   91
22. A Messiah Greater than Jonah and Solomon
        (Matthew 12:22–42)   95
23. Revealing the Secrets of the Kingdom (Matthew 13:1–23)   99
24. Parables of the Kingdom (Matthew 13:24–53)   103
Suggestions for Facilitators, Group Session 5   107

LESSONS 25–30

25. Rejection of Jesus and Execution of His Messenger
        (Matthew 14:1–12)   108
26. The Messiah Feeds the Multitudes and Walks on the Sea
        (Matthew 14:13–33)   111
27. Dispute Over What Pollutes a Person (Matthew 15:1–20)   115
28. Jesus Continues to Heal and Feed Many (Matthew 15:21–39)   118
29. The Leaven of the Pharisees and Sadducees
        (Matthew 16:1–12)   122
30. Peter Confesses that Jesus Is the Messiah (Matthew 16:13–28)   125
Suggestions for Facilitators, Group Session 6   130

The Gospel of Matthew in the Sunday Lectionary   131

How to Use
Threshold Bible Study

Threshold Bible Study is a dynamic, informative, inspiring, and life-changing series that helps you learn about Scripture in a whole new way. Each book will help you explore new dimensions of faith and discover deeper insights for your life as a disciple of Jesus.

The threshold is a place of transition. The threshold of God's word invites you to enter that place where God's truth, goodness, and beauty can shine into your life and fill your mind and heart. Through the Holy Spirit, the threshold becomes holy ground, sacred space, and graced time. God can teach you best at the threshold, because God opens your life to his word and fills you with the Spirit of truth.

With Threshold Bible Study each topic or book of the Bible is approached in a thematic way. You will understand and reflect on the biblical texts through overarching themes derived from biblical theology. Through this method, the study of Scripture will impact your life in a unique way and transform you from within.

These books are designed for maximum flexibility. Each study is presented in a workbook format, with sections for reading, reflecting, writing, discussing, and praying. Each Threshold book contains thirty lessons, which you can use for your daily study over the course of a month or which can be divided into six lessons per week, providing a group study of six weekly sessions. These studies are ideal for Bible study groups, small Christian communities, adult faith formation, student groups, Sunday school, neighborhood groups, and family reading, as well as for individual learning.

The commentary that follows each biblical passage launches your reflection on that passage and helps you begin to see its significance within the context of your contemporary experience. The questions following the commentary challenge you to understand the passage more fully and apply it to your own life. Space for writing after each question is ideal for personal study and also allows group participants to prepare for the weekly discussion. The prayer helps conclude your study each day by integrating your learning into your relationship with God.

The method of Threshold Bible Study is rooted in the ancient tradition of *lectio divina*, whereby studying the Bible becomes a means of deeper intimacy with

God and a transformed life. Reading and interpreting the text (*lectio*) is followed by reflective meditation on its message (*meditatio*). This reading and reflecting flows into prayer from the heart (*oratio* and *contemplatio*). In this way, one listens to God through the Scripture and then responds to God in prayer.

This ancient method assures you that Bible study is a matter of both the mind and the heart. It is not just an intellectual exercise to learn more and be able to discuss the Bible with others. It is, more importantly, a transforming experience. Reflecting on God's word, guided by the Holy Spirit, illumines the mind with wisdom and stirs the heart with zeal.

Following the personal Bible study, Threshold Bible Study offers ways to extend personal *lectio divina* into a weekly conversation with others. This communal experience will allow participants to enhance their appreciation of the message and build up a spiritual community (*collatio*). The end result will be to increase not only individual faith, but also faithful witness in the context of daily life (*operatio*).

When bringing Threshold Bible Study to a church community, try to make every effort to include as many people as possible. Many will want to study on their own; others will want to study with family, a group of friends, or a few work associates; some may want to commit themselves to share insights through a weekly conference call, daily text messaging, or an online social network; and others will want to gather weekly in established small groups.

By encouraging Threshold Bible Study and respecting the many ways people desire to make Bible study a regular part of their lives, you will widen the number of people in your church community who study the Bible regularly in whatever way they are able in their busy lives. Simply sign up people at the Sunday services and order bulk quantities for your church. Encourage people to follow the daily study as faithfully as they can through Sunday announcements, notices in parish publications, support on the church website, and other creative invitations and motivations.

Through the spiritual disciplines of Scripture reading, study, reflection, conversation, and prayer, Threshold Bible Study will help you experience God's grace more abundantly and root your life more deeply in Christ. The risen Jesus said: "Listen! I am standing at the door, knocking; if you hear my voice and open the door, I will come in to you and eat with you, and you with me" (Rev 3:20). Listen to the Word of God, open the door, and cross the threshold to an unimaginable dwelling with God!

SUGGESTIONS FOR INDIVIDUAL STUDY

• Make your Bible reading a time of prayer. Ask for God's guidance as you read the Scriptures.

• Try to study daily, or as often as possible according to the circumstances of your life.

• Read the Bible passage carefully, trying to understand both its meaning and its personal application as you read. Some persons find it helpful to read the passage aloud.

• Read the passage in another Bible translation. Each version adds to your understanding of the original text.

• Allow the commentary to help you comprehend and apply the scriptural text. The commentary is only a beginning, not the last word on the meaning of the passage.

• After reflecting on each question, write out your responses. The very act of writing will help you clarify your thoughts, bring new insights, and amplify your understanding.

• As you reflect on your answers, think about how you can live God's word in the context of your daily life.

• Conclude each daily lesson by reading the prayer and continuing with your own prayer from the heart.

• Make sure your reflections and prayers are matters of both the mind and the heart. A true encounter with God's word is always a transforming experience.

• Choose a word or a phrase from the lesson to carry with you throughout the day as a reminder of your encounter with God's life-changing word.

• Share your learning experience with at least one other person whom you trust for additional insights and affirmation. The ideal way to share learning is in a small group that meets regularly.

SUGGESTIONS FOR GROUP STUDY

• Meet regularly; weekly is ideal. Try to be on time and make attendance a high priority for the sake of the group. The average group meets for about an hour.

• Open each session with a prepared prayer, a song, or a reflection. Find some appropriate way to bring the group from the workaday world into a sacred time of graced sharing.

• If you have not been together before, name tags are very helpful as group members begin to become acquainted with one another.

• Spend the first session getting acquainted with one another, reading the Introduction aloud and discussing the questions that follow.

• Appoint a group facilitator to provide guidance to the discussion. The role of facilitator may rotate among members each week. The facilitator simply keeps the discussion on track; each person shares responsibility for the group. There is no need for the facilitator to be a trained teacher.

• Try to study the six lessons on your own during the week. When you have done your own reflection and written your own answers, you will be better prepared to discuss the six scriptural lessons with the group. If you have not had an opportunity to study the passages during the week, meet with the group anyway to share support and insights.

• Participate in the discussion as much as you are able, offering your thoughts, insights, feelings, and decisions. You learn by sharing with others the fruits of your study.

• Be careful not to dominate the discussion. It is important that everyone in the group be offered an equal opportunity to share the results of their work. Try to link what you say to the comments of others so that the group remains on the topic.

• When discussing your own personal thoughts or feelings, use "I" language. Be as personal and honest as appropriate and be very cautious about giving advice to others.

• Listen attentively to the other members of the group so as to learn from their insights. The words of the Bible affect each person in a different way, so a group provides a wealth of understanding for each member.

• Don't fear silence. Silence in a group is as important as silence in personal study. It allows individuals time to listen to the voice of God's Spirit and the opportunity to form their thoughts before they speak.

• Solicit several responses for each question. The thoughts of different people will build on the answers of others and will lead to deeper insights for all.

• Don't fear controversy. Differences of opinions are a sign of a healthy and honest group. If you cannot resolve an issue, continue on, agreeing to disagree. There is probably some truth in each viewpoint.

• Discuss the questions that seem most important for the group. There is no need to cover all the questions in the group session.

• Realize that some questions about the Bible cannot be resolved, even by experts. Don't get stuck on some issue for which there are no clear answers.

• Whatever is said in the group is said in confidence and should be regarded as such.

• Pray as a group in whatever way feels comfortable. Pray for the members of your group throughout the week.

Schedule for Group Study

Session 1: Introduction   Date: _____

Session 2: Lessons 1–6   Date: _____

Session 3: Lessons 7–12   Date: _____

Session 4: Lessons 13–18   Date: _____

Session 5: Lessons 19–24   Date: _____

Session 6: Lessons 25–30   Date: _____

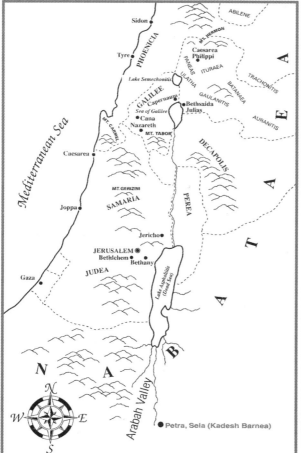

**As you go, proclaim the good news,
"The kingdom of heaven has come near."** Matt 10:7

Jesus, the Messianic King (Part 1)

The Gospel According to Matthew, the first book of the New Testament, is a proclamation of the good news of Jesus from the church of the first century. It testifies to the fact that what God has revealed through the events and writings of Israel's history has come to its completion in the life, death, and resurrection of Jesus. He himself is *the* gospel, the proclamation of God's good tidings. Jesus is the answer to God's promises revealed through the centuries of ancient Israel.

The more we study the Bible, the more we realize how exquisitely it all fits together, how each part is essential to the whole. We see how important it is that we have four gospels instead of one, how each complements the others by showing us a unique portrait of Jesus. The more we study the gospels, the more we realize how they grow out of the Old Testament, how the ancient Scriptures are filled with anticipation of the One to Come. The meaning and significance of the life of Jesus are seen in and through the Scriptures of Israel.

It should not be surprising that Matthew's gospel is significantly different from the other three gospels. Jesus did not demand from his followers a precise accounting of his deeds or a verbatim repetition of his teachings. He wanted from them a personal understanding of himself and his mission. So Matthew, like the other evangelists, used the oral and written traditions he received from others to form his own unique account of the good news of Jesus. He creatively structured and rewrote the material to meet the special needs of the community to which he wrote.

The way Matthew selected, shaped, and arranged the materials he received to form his gospel can tell us something about the setting and audience to which he wrote. The most obvious aspect of this gospel is its Jewish perspective. Its author was a Jewish Christian who wrote within a community that was mostly, though not exclusively, composed of Jews who believed in Jesus. The frequent quotations from the Hebrew Scriptures and the references throughout to Jewish practices indicate a community that was concerned with the meaning of Jesus' life in the context of the tradition of Israel. The gospel was written largely to help Jewish Christians understand that their faith in Jesus was entirely consistent with their Jewish heritage.

In trying to determine this gospel's place of origin, the evidence from the gospel itself is helpful in placing it most likely at Antioch in Syria. Here was the largest Jewish population outside of Palestine, which accounts for the Jewish Christian community as well as its Jewish opponents. There was also a sizable Gentile population, which accounts for the favorable comments about the Gentiles throughout the gospel. Antioch was a place where Greek was commonly used, and we know from the Acts of the Apostles that Jewish Christians from Jerusalem established a church there. As one of the most important cities of the Roman Empire, Antioch was the ideal place from which the gospel could be spread to "all the nations" (28:19).

The primary conflict within Judaism at the time of Matthew's writing concerned how Judaism would continue to exist after the destruction of Jerusalem's temple by the Romans in A.D. 70. One popular response to this issue was rabbinical Judaism, which developed from the tradition of the Pharisees and the scribes. This movement centered around the synagogues and was concerned with living out the Torah in the ways in which the rabbis were interpreting it. Another response to this conflict was Jewish Christianity. The community of Matthew claimed that the messianic movement begun in Jesus was the most authentic way of living out the tradition of Israel in the latter decades of the first century and beyond. For this reason, the Gospel of Matthew demonstrated that the life of Jesus was the fulfillment of the Hebrew

Scriptures and that Jesus is the most authoritative interpreter of Israel's Torah.

Reflection and Discussion

• What might be some reasons why the Gospel of Matthew was chosen by the church as the first book of the New Testament?

• What seem to be some of the characteristic features of this gospel that distinguish it from the other gospels?

Jesus as the Messiah, the Son of David, the Son of Abraham

The gospel offers us the most important titles or descriptors of Jesus' identity in the first verse: "An account of the genealogy of Jesus the Messiah, the son of David, the son of Abraham." These three titles of Jesus are the key to Matthew's expression of Jesus' identity in this gospel. Each of these is a royal title within the tradition of Israel and links Jesus with Israel's history and with all the hopes of God's people.

"Messiah" is the Hebrew word for the "anointed" of God; it is *Christos* in Greek. The word originally referred to one designated by God for a chosen role, such as a king (Psalm 2:2), priest (Lev 4:3), or prophet (1 Kings 19:16). In later writings, Messiah was a royal title, designating a future ruler who would play a decisive role in fulfilling God's plans for Israel. Based on prophecies given to King David, the Messiah to come would free God's people from oppression and usher in a new age. The gospel will clarify what it means to call Jesus the Messiah, the Christ.

"Son of David" is a messianic title used frequently for Jesus throughout the gospel. It highlights the fact that the Messiah was to come from the royal line of King David. He would be a descendant of David to whom God had promised an everlasting reign (2 Sam 7:12–16). This Son of David would use his royal power to heal the needy and to bring about God's rule of justice upon his people. His messianic reign would be revealed not through force and conquest but through self-sacrificial love and service.

"Son of Abraham" links Jesus with the beginning of God's covenant with Israel, a covenant initiated with Abraham. Abraham is the father of all believers, the head of Israel's royal lineage leading to David and Jesus. The title portrays Jesus as the one who culminates God's plans that originated in Abraham. God had pledged to Abraham that his call and obedience would benefit all the peoples and nations of the earth (Gen 12:3; 22:18). As Son of Abraham, what God accomplishes in Jesus fulfills that promise for the whole human race.

The word translated "genealogy" in the gospel's first verse is the Greek word *genesis*. It may also be translated as "beginning," or "origin." It is quite possible that Matthew chose the word "genesis" for his gospel's opening verse to evoke associations with the first book of the Bible. As Genesis is about the origins of creation, humanity, and Israel, so Jesus is a new beginning for creation, humanity, and Israel. What God is doing in Jesus the Messiah is a fresh, definitive, creative action for the sake of the world. All that God had planned and promised throughout the Scriptures is fulfilled in the coming of Jesus Christ.

Reflection and Discussion

• Why is a familiarity with the Old Testament so helpful in understanding Matthew's gospel?

• Why is it so important that the origins of Jesus be connected with both Abraham and David?

The True King Who Establishes His Kingdom

After Matthew's gospel begins by linking Jesus with the royal line of David, its infancy account demonstrates that Jesus is born to be king. As Israel's anointed one, Jesus is the royal Messiah to whom the prophecies point. His entry into Jerusalem toward the end of his life is the action of a king. In the gospel Jesus is given these royal titles: Messiah, Son of David, King of the Jews, King of Israel, and Son of God. In the person of Jesus Christ, the divine kingship, asserted throughout the Old Testament, and the human kingship, exemplified in David, finally and uniquely merge. In the final scene of the gospel, Jesus declares, "All authority in heaven and on earth has been given to me."

As God's anointed, Jesus brings the kingdom of God to the sphere of human experience. God's kingdom is at the center of his preaching ministry: "Repent, for the kingdom of heaven has come near" (4:17). Matthew refers to the divine reign more often as the "kingdom of heaven" than as the "kingdom of God." This is due either to his Jewish reverence for the name of God or to emphasize that it is the kingdom of both the Father and the Son. The miracles of Jesus demonstrate that Jesus brings the kingdom near and makes it effective in the lives of individuals. His parables illustrate the paradoxical nature of the kingdom and its distinctive aspects. The teachings of Jesus present the lifestyle and mindset of one who lives in view of the kingdom's coming and they demonstrate the childlike trust required to enter God's reign. The royal power of God is dynamically present in Jesus' words and deeds.

The gospel presents the kingdom of heaven as both present and future. In the present, Jesus' healings, exorcisms, and miracles reveal the transforming power of the kingdom breaking into human history and defeating the enslaving control of evil, sin, and death. The kingdom has been inaugurated in the coming of Jesus and will be consummated in his glorious return. What we experience now in microcosm through the presence of Jesus living in his church, we will one day experience in macrocosm when Christ reigns over all creation and the oppressive powers of evil, sin, and death are thoroughly vanquished. The gospel demonstrates that Jesus is God's kingdom in person. While we live in hope of the future, God's kingdom has come upon us in the life, death, and resurrection of the messianic King.

Reflection and Discussion

• What aspects of the kingship of Jesus make it uniquely different from the rule of this world's kings?

• In what sense can we say that the Gospel of Matthew is all about the coming of God's kingdom?

The Unique Content of Matthew's Gospel

Matthew's description of a Christian scribe, as one who "brings out of his treasure what is new and what is old" (13:52), may be an autobiographical statement about how he sees his role as an evangelist. For, more than any other gospel writer, Matthew presents references to God's word and work in the Old Testament and places them in relation to God's new word and work in Jesus Christ. This unique presentation of the old and the new makes

Matthew's gospel the ideal, first book of the New Testament. His presentation of the good news is the entryway from the ancient covenant to the new, the threshold leading the believer from the history of Israel into the proclamation to all the nations.

One of Matthew's most notable characteristics as a writer is his enrichment of the text with numerous quotations from the Old Testament. In conjunction with a quote, the writer usually states that the life of Jesus is a fulfillment of what was spoken through the ancient text. Yet, beyond these obvious quotations, the writer alludes to many other words, images, or events from the Hebrew Scriptures. Through the use of such references, Matthew demonstrates his conviction that the saving life of Jesus is accomplishing the ancient promises of God.

One unique characteristic of this gospel is the way the evangelist gathers the various teachings of Jesus into five blocks of teaching. These great discourses are the sermon on the mount (Mt 5–7), the sermon to the apostles (Mt 10), the sermon on the kingdom (Mt 13), the sermon on leadership (Mt 18), and the sermon on the last things (Mt 24–25). These five discourses have been compared to the five books of Moses, which compose the Torah of Israel. With these five sermons, Jesus instructs his disciples and his church, and as his disciples and as his church, we sit at the feet of Jesus and listen to his teachings in order to be formed for the kingdom.

By presenting Jesus as the authoritative teacher of his church, this gospel helped Jewish Christians understand how to be loyal to the old covenant with Moses while engaging with Gentile believers. It confirmed the community's continuity with God's past promises to Israel while also validating the members' new loyalty to Jesus and his saving mission. As such, the gospel became an effective pastoral tool for the church's preaching, teaching, and worship. In every age it has brought direction and hope for Christ's disciples, inviting them into an ever deeper relationship with Jesus, who promises to remain always with his church.

Our study of the Gospel of Matthew is divided into roughly two halves. The first half, chapters 1 through 16, leads up to the profession of Peter and to Jesus' announcement of his own coming suffering, death, and resurrection. The second half, chapters 17 through 28, follows the journey of Jesus with his disciples to Jerusalem, where he will experience the climactic moments of his saving ministry. Through the study of this gospel, we will experience the saving news of Jesus as it was experienced by that early community of Jews and Gentiles to which Matthew addressed his gospel. As the gospel equipped those ancient Christians with the teaching of Jesus the Messiah so they could spread the message of the kingdom to all the nations, the gospel will prepare us with the transforming experience of Jesus Christ to be bearers of the good news in the world today.

Reflection and Discussion

• Keeping in mind the Jewish context and audience of Matthew's gospel, how do I understand the importance of the Jewish tradition for my appreciation of Jesus?

• In what way do I want to draw closer to Jesus as I study the Gospel of Matthew?

Prayer

Creating and Redeeming God, you prepared the people of Israel with hope for the coming of the Messiah. In the coming of Jesus you brought your ancient promises to fulfillment and opened salvation to all the nations of the world. Stir up within me a deep desire to know Jesus Christ more fully and to listen carefully to his teachings. Enlighten and encourage me as I read and contemplate your inspired word in these sacred Scriptures. Show me how to make my life a testimony to the presence of your kingdom.

SUGGESTIONS FOR FACILITATORS, GROUP SESSION 1

1. If the group is meeting for the first time, or if there are newcomers joining the group, it is helpful to provide name tags.

2. Distribute the books to the members of the group.

3. You may want to ask the participants to introduce themselves and tell the group a bit about themselves.

4. Ask one or more of these introductory questions:
   - What drew you to join this group?
   - What is your biggest fear in beginning this Bible study?
   - How is beginning this study like a "threshold" for you?

5. You may want to pray this prayer as a group:

Come upon us, Holy Spirit, to enlighten and guide us as we begin this study of Matthew's gospel. You inspired the writers of the Scriptures to reveal your presence throughout the history of salvation. This inspired word has the power to convert our hearts and change our lives. Fill our hearts with desire, trust, and confidence as you shine the light of your truth within us. Motivate us to read the Scriptures and give us a deeper love for God's word each day. Bless us during this session and throughout the coming week with the fire of your love.

6. Read the Introduction aloud, pausing at each question for discussion. Group members may wish to write the insights of the group as each question is discussed. Encourage several members of the group to respond to each question.

7. Don't feel compelled to finish the complete Introduction during the session. It is better to allow sufficient time to talk about the questions raised than to rush to the end. Group members may read any remaining sections on their own after the group meeting.

8. Instruct group members to read the first six lessons on their own during the six days before the next group meeting. They should write out their own answers to the questions as preparation for next week's group discussion.

9. Fill in the date for each group meeting under "Schedule for Group Study."

10. Conclude by praying aloud together the prayer at the end of the Introduction.

...and Jacob the father of Joseph the husband of Mary, of whom Jesus was born, who is called the Messiah. Matt 1:16

Descendant of Abraham and David

MATTHEW 1:1–17 ¹*An account of the genealogy of Jesus the Messiah, the son of David, the son of Abraham.*

²*Abraham was the father of Isaac, and Isaac the father of Jacob, and Jacob the father of Judah and his brothers,* ³*and Judah the father of Perez and Zerah by Tamar, and Perez the father of Hezron, and Hezron the father of Aram,* ⁴*and Aram the father of Aminadab, and Aminadab the father of Nahshon, and Nahshon the father of Salmon,* ⁵*and Salmon the father of Boaz by Rahab, and Boaz the father of Obed by Ruth, and Obed the father of Jesse,* ⁶*and Jesse the father of King David.*

And David was the father of Solomon by the wife of Uriah, ⁷*and Solomon the father of Rehoboam, and Rehoboam the father of Abijah, and Abijah the father of Asaph,* ⁸*and Asaph the father of Jehoshaphat, and Jehoshaphat the father of Joram, and Joram the father of Uzziah,* ⁹*and Uzziah the father of Jotham, and Jotham the father of Ahaz, and Ahaz the father of Hezekiah,* ¹⁰*and Hezekiah the father of Manasseh, and Manasseh the father of Amos, and Amos the father of Josiah,* ¹¹*and Josiah the father of Jechoniah and his brothers, at the time of the deportation to Babylon.*

¹²*And after the deportation to Babylon: Jechoniah was the father of Salathiel, and Salathiel the father of Zerubbabel,* ¹³*and Zerubbabel the father of Abiud, and Abiud the father of Eliakim, and Eliakim the father of Azor,* ¹⁴*and Azor the father of Zadok, and Zadok the father of Achim, and Achim the father of Eliud,* ¹⁵*and Eliud the father of Eleazar, and Eleazar the father of Matthan, and Matthan the father of Jacob,* ¹⁶*and Jacob the father of Joseph the husband of Mary, of whom Jesus was born, who is called the Messiah.*

¹⁷*So all the generations from Abraham to David are fourteen generations; and from David to the deportation to Babylon, fourteen generations; and from the deportation to Babylon to the Messiah, fourteen generations.*

The gospel's opening passage links the coming of the Messiah with the ancient history of the people of Israel. Jesus is connected with the long list of names, going back to the earliest history of God's covenant with his chosen people. As the culmination of this long history, Jesus is shown to be the achievement of Israel's highest hopes, the one for whom that ancient tradition has prepared.

Biblical genealogies are rarely concerned with mere biological descent. The writer carefully constructed this genealogy to show salvation history divided into three great epochs. The first period begins with Abraham and ascends to the high point of Israel's ancient history, the kingship of David (verses 2–6). Within this period, Jesus is shown to be related to the great patriarchs of Israel, including not only Judah but "his brothers." The twelve sons of Jacob connect Jesus to the whole of Israel, the twelve tribes that will be called to the kingdom by the twelve apostles of Jesus. Like the monarchy of David, which first joined the tribes together and confirmed their united destiny in the kingdom of Israel, the reign of Jesus will unite all of God's people into the unity of God's kingdom.

The second period begins with King David and descends to the low point of Israel's history, the exile in Babylon (verses 7–11). Here is a list of mostly corrupt Judean kings, described in the Hebrew Scriptures as murderers, idolaters, and adulterers. Only Hezekiah and Josiah are described as faithful to God's covenant and offer hope for the future. By the time of the exile, the people's expectation of a saving king seemed like a distant dream.

The third period begins with the exile in Babylon and ascends again to the goal of Israel's history, the coming of the Messiah (verses 12–16). Many Jews of Jesus' day considered Israel still in exile, awaiting the restoration of David's dynasty by the Messiah. This pattern of fourteen generations in each epoch emphasizes the two climactic points, the reign of David and the coming of Christ, the long-awaited ruler who would fulfill God's promises to David (verse 17). The number fourteen relates to the numerical value of "David" in Hebrew (d-w-d = 4+6+4). It was common also for the Jews to divide time into periods of sevens. According to this configuration, Jesus was preceded by six periods of seven generations (three times fourteen), and the reign of the Messiah opened the seventh period of seven, the period of fullness and completion. This fixed pattern indicates that the coming of Christ marked the culmination of God's careful plan.

The inclusion of four women—Tamar, Rahab, Ruth, and the wife of Uriah (Bathsheba)—is unusual, since women were not normally included in genealogies. Each of them seems an unlikely choice to be included in the messianic lineage. They were all in some sense outsiders—sinners, outcasts, or foreigners—whom God used to carry forward his saving purposes. Their inclusion, among all the many corrupt and scandalous men in the genealogy, prepared for the ministry of Jesus in which sinners, outcasts, and ultimately Gentiles, enter the kingdom. The universal gospel breaks down the barriers between Jew and Gentile, male and female, sinner and saint.

This genealogy writes the fathers and mothers of Israel into the family tree of Christians. Lest we think of this genealogy as merely a monotonous list of unpronounceable names, we are reminded very specifically that our identity in Christ is rooted in the memory of our ancestors in the Hebrew Scriptures. The history of Jesus did not begin in Nazareth or Bethlehem, for it contains the stories of ancient patriarchs, prophets, kings, and generations of men and women leading up to "Joseph the husband of Mary, of whom Jesus was born" (verse 16).

Reflection and Discussion

• What is the significance of dividing Israel's history into three epochs of fourteen generations each?

• In what way does the inclusion of women in the genealogy prepare for the inclusive ministry of Jesus?

• How does the end of the genealogy (verse 16) indicate the relationship of Joseph and Mary to the lineage of Jesus? How does the way Mary is included prepare for the account of Jesus' birth?

• What evidence is there in the genealogy and in my life that God works in unexpected ways?

Prayer

God of our ancestors, from Abraham, through David, to Joseph and Mary, you prepared the world for the coming of Christ. Help me to honor the spiritual legacy of my ancestors, and make my life a new witness in your saving plan for the world.

"Look, the virgin shall conceive and bear a son, and they shall name him Emmanuel," which means, "God is with us." Matt 1:23

The Messiah's Royal Birth

MATTHEW 1:18–25 ¹⁸*Now the birth of Jesus the Messiah took place in this way. When his mother Mary had been engaged to Joseph, but before they lived together, she was found to be with child from the Holy Spirit.* ¹⁹*Her husband Joseph, being a righteous man and unwilling to expose her to public disgrace, planned to dismiss her quietly.* ²⁰*But just when he had resolved to do this, an angel of the Lord appeared to him in a dream and said, "Joseph, son of David, do not be afraid to take Mary as your wife, for the child conceived in her is from the Holy Spirit.* ²¹*She will bear a son, and you are to name him Jesus, for he will save his people from their sins."* ²²*All this took place to fulfill what had been spoken by the Lord through the prophet:*

²³*"Look, the virgin shall conceive and bear a son,*
    and they shall name him Emmanuel,"

which means, "God is with us." ²⁴*When Joseph awoke from sleep, he did as the angel of the Lord commanded him; he took her as his wife,* ²⁵*but had no marital relations with her until she had borne a son; and he named him Jesus.*

The birth narrative carries forward the theme that Jesus is the promised Messiah who will restore his people and bring them salvation. Matthew explains how the coming Messiah would be both Son of

David and Son of God. Through the lineage of Joseph and his legal paternity, Jesus is Son of David; through the Holy Spirit and the virginal maternity of Mary, he is Son of God. The obedient responses of both Joseph and Mary to the divine will were necessary for Christ's coming into the world. Through Joseph, Jesus' birth is placed in continuity with God's work through the ages, thus expressing God's consistent faithfulness; through Mary, his birth is shown to be a marvelously new divine action, thus expressing God's astonishing creativity.

The angel evokes the messianic prophecies of the future king by calling Joseph "son of David" (verse 20). Though not the biological father of Jesus, Joseph becomes the legal, adoptive father of Jesus by bringing Mary into his home in marriage, assuming public responsibility for the child, and by naming his child. Jesus becomes a legitimate descendant of David's royal lineage because his lawful, adoptive father was from the line of David. Through Joseph, Jesus could be proclaimed as the Son of David, the Messiah of Israel.

Joseph's choices were agonizing. Mary and Joseph were "betrothed," a legally binding relationship for a year or more before the couple were to share the same home. The evidence spoke for itself. Joseph could only assume that Mary had relations with another man. Yet Joseph, out of love for Mary, chose to quietly divorce her, without public accusation, trial, punishment, and shame. Yet the revelation in his dream cut short one painful choice and presented him with another: the choice to cooperate with the inconceivable grace of God. The angel revealed that the conception of the child in Mary was "from the Holy Spirit" (verses 18, 20). In the Hebrew Scriptures, the spirit of God was linked with God's creating power, the words of the prophets, and God's renewal of creation in the last days. Because Joseph followed God's will, his life entered the cosmic drama wherein heaven and earth met in the child of Mary's womb.

The first of Matthew's quotations from the Hebrew Scriptures is from Isaiah 7:14, the Emmanuel prophecy (verse 23). Proclaimed by Isaiah in the eighth century before Christ, the words formed an oracle of hope that assured the continuance of David's dynasty after a period of devastation. It spoke of the birth of a king who would bring restoration to the kingdom and be a sign that God was truly with his people. Because this prophecy did not find satisfactory fulfillment in the generations immediately following its announcement, its high ideals became a messianic hope for a future age.

Matthew and his Jewish Christian community came to understand that the words of Isaiah were being accomplished through the pregnancy of Mary and the pending birth of Israel's messianic king (verse 22). The royal Savior born of the Virgin Mary fully manifested God's faithful presence. In his royal birth and the good news of salvation, the church knew that "God is with us."

Reflection and Discussion

• What parts of this passage indicate continuity between the Old and New Testaments? What parts indicate a surprising break between the Old and New?

• What do I admire most about Joseph? In what way could Joseph be a mentor for my life?

• What did Emmanuel, "God is with us," mean to Isaiah? What did it mean for Matthew in his birth narrative? What does it mean today as I seek to follow Christ?

Prayer

Jesus, Emmanuel, you were born into the world as a manifestation that God is with us. Help me believe that God is with me in the best and worst of times. Renew my hope in your promises and give me trust, like Joseph, to live with confidence.

They saw the child with Mary his mother; and they knelt down and paid him homage. Then, opening their treasure chests, they offered him gifts of gold, frankincense, and myrrh. Matt 2:11

Homage and Gifts for the King

MATTHEW 2:1–12 ¹*In the time of King Herod, after Jesus was born in Bethlehem of Judea, wise men from the East came to Jerusalem,* ²*asking, "Where is the child who has been born king of the Jews? For we observed his star at its rising, and have come to pay him homage."* ³*When King Herod heard this, he was frightened, and all Jerusalem with him;* ⁴*and calling together all the chief priests and scribes of the people, he inquired of them where the Messiah was to be born.* ⁵*They told him, "In Bethlehem of Judea; for so it has been written by the prophet:*

⁶*'And you, Bethlehem, in the land of Judah,*
are by no means least among the rulers of Judah;
for from you shall come a ruler
who is to shepherd my people Israel.'"

⁷*Then Herod secretly called for the wise men and learned from them the exact time when the star had appeared.* ⁸*Then he sent them to Bethlehem, saying, "Go and search diligently for the child; and when you have found him, bring me word so that I may also go and pay him homage."* ⁹*When they had heard the king, they set out; and there, ahead of them, went the star that they had seen at its rising,*

until it stopped over the place where the child was. [10] *When they saw that the star had stopped, they were overwhelmed with joy.* [11] *On entering the house, they saw the child with Mary his mother; and they knelt down and paid him homage. Then, opening their treasure chests, they offered him gifts of gold, frankincense, and myrrh.* [12] *And having been warned in a dream not to return to Herod, they left for their own country by another road.*

Because of the widespread expectation among the Jewish people of a coming messianic ruler, King Herod saw the news of a newborn king as a threat to his own power, and conflict became inevitable. He had taken upon himself the illegitimate title "King of the Jews" as well as assumed the prerogative of a royal son of David by rebuilding the temple in Jerusalem. His reign was noted for its murderous cruelty, and he was insanely distrustful of any perceived threats to his power. His apparent interest in the child was deceitful, for he intended to destroy Jesus, not pay homage to him.

The "chief priests and scribes of the people" know the ancient prophecies that the Messiah was to be born in Bethlehem, the ancestral city of King David (verses 4–5). The prophetic text is a quote from Micah stating that although Bethlehem is small, the town's stature is now great because the Messiah has been born there (verse 6). The last line of the quotation refers to the anointing of David there many centuries before: "You shall be shepherd of my people Israel, you who shall rule over Israel" (2 Sam 5:2).

The wise men from the East, avid scholars of spiritual mysteries, undertook an arduous journey to honor the infant of whom great things were prophesied. Whether these seekers were from Persia, Arabia, Babylon, or other places to the East, their significance is that they were Gentiles from distant nations. Later tradition embellished the biblical account by giving names and royal titles to these magi: Melchior, king of Persia; Gaspar, king of India; and Balthasar, king of Arabia. The wise men interpreted the rising of the star as a heavenly sign marking the birth of a great ruler. In the days of Moses, a seer from the East named Balaam had blessed Israel's future by proclaiming a coming king who would be announced by a star: "A star shall come out of Jacob, and a scepter shall rise out of Israel" (Num 24:17). The text of the gospel states that the star was not just any unusual cosmic occurrence, but "his star," a divine sign pointing to the Messiah.

The scene sets up a stark contrast between the paranoid fear of King Herod and the adoring homage of the wise men. While Herod plots the death of the child, the strangers from the East kneel before the child and offer him gifts worthy of a king. Again we find allusions to ancient texts of Israel. Psalm 72 had proclaimed a son of David who would be honored by all the nations: "May the kings of Sheba and Seba bring gifts; May all kings fall down before him, all nations give him service" (Ps 72:10–11). Isaiah had announced that "All from Sheba shall come. They shall bring gold and frankincense, and shall proclaim the praise of the Lord" (Isa 60:6).

The Gentile magi who come to worship at Christ's birth anticipate all the believers from all the nations who will be called to salvation through this King from the line of David. For this Son of David is also Son of Abraham, in whom all the nations of the earth are destined to be blessed. The origins of Jesus point to his destiny. During his public ministry, some accepted him and did him homage; others rejected him and sought to put him to death. The disciples of Jesus would meet a similar reception when they proclaimed the gospel after the resurrection. Some people would accept the saving good news; others would oppose it and violently persecute the community of faith. From his birth, Jesus is destined to be the suffering Messiah whose worldwide dominion will bring salvation to all the nations.

Reflection and Discussion

• Why was King Herod so eager to put Jesus to death in his infancy?

• Why would the coming of the Messiah evoke such a violent response from some and such a welcome from others?

• What is the significance of the star for Matthew's gospel? What are the signs of Christ's presence that God offers to me?

• Why does Matthew choose to insert the story of the magi here? Whom do they represent in God's saving plan?

• Though the wise men were from outside the tradition of Judaism, their response demonstrated their acceptance of God's signs in the world. What can I learn about God from those outside my own religion?

Prayer

Lord of all the nations, you mark the path of my life with your shining light and you guide me on my journey to you. Give me the desire to kneel before you and present to you the gifts of my life.

When Herod died, an angel of the Lord suddenly appeared in a dream to Joseph in Egypt and said, "Get up, take the child and his mother, and go to the land of Israel, for those who were seeking the child's life are dead."

Matt 2:19–20

Escape to Egypt and Return to Israel

MATTHEW 2:13–23 ¹³*Now after they had left, an angel of the Lord appeared to Joseph in a dream and said, "Get up, take the child and his mother, and flee to Egypt, and remain there until I tell you; for Herod is about to search for the child, to destroy him." ¹⁴Then Joseph got up, took the child and his mother by night, and went to Egypt, ¹⁵and remained there until the death of Herod. This was to fulfill what had been spoken by the Lord through the prophet, "Out of Egypt I have called my son."*

¹⁶When Herod saw that he had been tricked by the wise men, he was infuriated, and he sent and killed all the children in and around Bethlehem who were two years old or under, according to the time that he had learned from the wise men. ¹⁷Then was fulfilled what had been spoken through the prophet Jeremiah:

¹⁸"A voice was heard in Ramah,
wailing and loud lamentation,
Rachel weeping for her children;
she refused to be consoled, because they are no more."

¹⁹*When Herod died, an angel of the Lord suddenly appeared in a dream to Joseph in Egypt and said,* ²⁰*"Get up, take the child and his mother, and go to the land of Israel, for those who were seeking the child's life are dead."* ²¹*Then Joseph got up, took the child and his mother, and went to the land of Israel.* ²²*But when he heard that Archelaus was ruling over Judea in place of his father Herod, he was afraid to go there. And after being warned in a dream, he went away to the district of Galilee.* ²³*There he made his home in a town called Nazareth, so that what had been spoken through the prophets might be fulfilled, "He will be called a Nazorean."*

The theme of God's purpose and divine providence permeates the narrative. The dreams of Joseph carry the story forward, confirming that God is orchestrating events, protecting his Messiah, and carrying forth his saving plan. This account of Joseph resembles the great epic of Joseph, the son of Jacob, in the book of Genesis (Gen 37–50). This ancient Joseph was known as a dreamer and an interpreter of dreams, and he saved his family from death by bringing them into Egypt. The New Testament Joseph relives the life of his ancestor through responding to dreams and traveling to Egypt to seek refuge for his family.

The coming of Jesus is not only a new genesis, but also a new exodus. Jesus' infancy echoes the stories of Moses' birth and childhood. In both accounts there is a decree from a wicked king (Pharaoh and Herod) to slaughter the male babies (Exod 1:15–16), but the chosen child escapes in a wondrous way (Exod 2:1–10) while the other innocent infants are killed (Exod 1:22). In both accounts there is a flight to a foreign land to escape the king's decree (Exod 2:15) and then a divinely directed return to the land after the king's death (Exod 4:19).

The rescue of the infant Moses from the wicked Pharaoh prepares for the liberation of God's people through the later ministry of Moses. Likewise, the rescue of Jesus from the sinister king prepares for his later ministry of redeeming his people. Jesus will leave Egypt, pass through the water in baptism, undergo trials and temptations in the desert, teach from the mountain, and establish the new covenant. He is the new Moses, the renewed Israel, the eternal covenant, the Savior of his people.

Each of the four episodes in the gospel's second chapter is related to a place associated with a key feature of salvation history. Bethlehem harks back to

God's choice of David (verses 1–12); Egypt recalls God's decision to free Israel from bondage (verses 13–15); Ramah is a reminder of Israel's captivity in Babylon (verses 16–18); Nazareth anticipates the life of Jesus (verses 19–23). The Old Testament citation helps us understand the events of the gospel more deeply by recalling the larger context of each episode from the history of God's salvation.

While Joseph carries the action forward through God's revelation in dreams, the center of attention is the child Jesus and his mother, Mary. Matthew repeats the phrase "the child and his mother" in each episode (verses 11, 13, 14, 20, 21). This focus on the messianic child along with his mother reflects the central role of the king's mother in the birth, enthronement, and reign of the kings in David's line. The book of Kings mentions the name of the king's mother in the introduction to each reign in Judah. She had an official position in the kingdom and often kept her position even after her son's death. The queen mother was enthroned with the king and enjoyed a position of great honor and dignity during his reign (1 Kings 2:19; Jer 13:18). Matthew's infancy account alludes to the role of the mother of the Messiah in the kingdom inaugurated by Jesus Christ.

In the final episode of Matthew's introductory narrative, Joseph is directed to take Jesus and Mary to Galilee and to settle in the town of Nazareth. Though Matthew sees this as one more way in which the Scriptures are fulfilled, there is actually no single text in the Old Testament that contains the words "He will be called a Nazorean" (verse 23). Most probably Matthew sees a wordplay with the Hebrew word *netzer*, which means "branch," and alludes to the prophet Isaiah: "A shoot shall come up from the stock of Jesse, and a branch shall grow out of his roots" (Isa 11:1). Matthew shows that Jesus is that branch growing from the root of Jesse, the father of King David, again highlighting Jesus' identity as the messianic king from the line of David.

Matthew demonstrates how the coming of Jesus is in continuity with all that has come before him, yet also how his coming is a completely new action of God. By looking back into ancient Israel and forward into the ministry of Jesus, the infancy narrative shows us how the new grows out of the old, and the old finds fuller expression in the new. We will now see how all the claims made for Jesus at his birth will be realized throughout his saving life and how Jesus the Nazorean is indeed the messianic king of God's people.

Reflection and Discussion

• In what ways does the gospel present Jesus as the new Moses?

• Why does the infancy account associate Jesus with some of the key places of Israel's history? What are the places where God has led me as part of his saving plan?

• Why does Matthew focus our attention on "the child and his mother" in each episode? Why is the child's mother significant for my understanding of Jesus?

Prayer

God of Israel and Father of Jesus, you guided and protected your Son with your loving care. Safeguard me and lead me to the places where I can best experience your presence and serve you.

"Prepare the way of the Lord, make his paths straight." Matt 3:3

God's Kingdom Is at Hand

MATTHEW 3:1–17 *¹In those days John the Baptist appeared in the wilderness of Judea, proclaiming, ²"Repent, for the kingdom of heaven has come near." ³This is the one of whom the prophet Isaiah spoke when he said,*

"The voice of one crying out in the wilderness:
'Prepare the way of the Lord,
make his paths straight.'"

⁴Now John wore clothing of camel's hair with a leather belt around his waist, and his food was locusts and wild honey. ⁵Then the people of Jerusalem and all Judea were going out to him, and all the region along the Jordan, ⁶and they were baptized by him in the river Jordan, confessing their sins.

⁷But when he saw many Pharisees and Sadducees coming for baptism, he said to them, "You brood of vipers! Who warned you to flee from the wrath to come? ⁸Bear fruit worthy of repentance. ⁹Do not presume to say to yourselves, 'We have Abraham as our ancestor'; for I tell you, God is able from these stones to raise up children to Abraham. ¹⁰Even now the ax is lying at the root of the trees; every tree therefore that does not bear good fruit is cut down and thrown into the fire.

¹¹"I baptize you with water for repentance, but one who is more powerful than I is coming after me; I am not worthy to carry his sandals. He will baptize

25

you with the Holy Spirit and fire. [12]*His winnowing fork is in his hand, and he will clear his threshing floor and will gather his wheat into the granary; but the chaff he will burn with unquenchable fire."*

[13]*Then Jesus came from Galilee to John at the Jordan, to be baptized by him.* [14]*John would have prevented him, saying, "I need to be baptized by you, and do you come to me?"* [15]*But Jesus answered him, "Let it be so now; for it is proper for us in this way to fulfill all righteousness." Then he consented.* [16]*And when Jesus had been baptized, just as he came up from the water, suddenly the heavens were opened to him and he saw the Spirit of God descending like a dove and alighting on him.* [17]*And a voice from heaven said, "This is my Son, the Beloved, with whom I am well pleased."*

The "wilderness of Judah" is the setting for the ministry of John the Baptist and the beginning of Jesus' public life. This barren area near the Dead Sea reminds us of the desert in which Israel experienced the trial and testing of the exodus. John's command, "Repent, for the kingdom of heaven has come near," is the same as Jesus' opening proclamation in Galilee (4:17). Repentance entails a radical conversion to a new way of life, a turning of the whole person away from sin and toward God. It demands an interior change of heart, a deeply rooted decision, and a consequent lifestyle of obedience to God.

The call to repentance is based on the reality that God's kingdom has drawn near. "The kingdom of heaven" is Matthew's way of referring to the kingdom of God without mentioning the name of God. This kingdom should not be thought of as a place or a physical entity. Rather, the kingdom is God's kingly rule or reign. The demand for repentance is urgent because, in the divine redemptive plan, the reign of God is at hand—it is imminent.

The ministry of John the Baptist is shown to fulfill the words of the prophet Isaiah (verse 3). In their historical context, the words of Isaiah gave comfort to the exiles in Babylon with the hope of their return to the land. In their wider context, the prophetic words prepare for the final restoration of Israel and its results for all humanity. As a consequence of preparing "the way of the Lord," Isaiah proclaims, "Then the glory of the Lord shall be revealed, and all people shall see it together" (Isa 40:3–5). John's voice in the wilderness prepares for the coming of God's universal salvation. He is shown to be the new

Elijah, the ancient prophet who was expected to return as the precursor of these final days (Mal 3:1; 4:5). His austere clothing and diet are much like Elijah of old and reflect the urgent message he preaches (verse 4).

The baptism John offers in the Jordan River signifies the repentance he preaches. The response to John's message is overwhelmingly positive. Yet when the religious leaders, the Pharisees and Sadducees, arrive, John denounces their insincerity and offers three stern warnings. First, he insists that repentance must be accompanied by visible evidence in the form of good deeds (verse 8). Second, he warns against thinking that birth into the people of God is sufficient for salvation (verse 9). Third, he urges them not to waste the little time that is still available to show evidence of a repentant lifestyle (verse 10).

Though John and Jesus proclaim the same message, their missions are quite different. John is the forerunner, preparing for Jesus with a water baptism of repentance. Jesus will baptize "with the Holy Spirit and fire" (verse 11). Both cleansing water and refining fire are prophetic images expressing the outpouring of God's Spirit in the final age. This baptismal expression of Jesus' work refers to his whole ministry of preaching, healing, and forgiving. His ministry is like a harvester who separates the wheat from the chaff by tossing the harvested grain in the air with a winnowing fork (verse 12). The righteous are like the good wheat gathered into the granary while the unrepentant are like the useless chaff to be swept up and burnt.

When Jesus comes for baptism, John protests his unworthiness to baptize Jesus. But Jesus is baptized in order to exemplify the righteousness asked of all God's people. Though he has no reason to repent of sin, he personifies the ideal Israel in relationship to God. The heavenly vision expresses the descent of God's Spirit upon him (verse 16). The heavenly voice expresses God's approval of Jesus as his Son. As God had described Israel as his "firstborn son" (Exod 4:22), that filial relationship between God and Israel is now personified and fulfilled in Jesus.

Reflection and Discussion

• What is the essence of John's call to repentance? Why does he use the image of a fruitful tree to signify a repentant life?

• What warning of judgment do I need to hear from the preaching of John? What fruit of repentance is God asking of me?

• Why did Jesus insist on being baptized by John, though he was sinless? What does this teach me about him?

Prayer

Father, you prepared the world for the coming of your Son through John the Baptist's call to repentance. Help me to turn away from sin and turn my heart to you so that I may bear fruit worthy of your kingdom.

From that time Jesus began to proclaim,
"Repent, for the kingdom of heaven has come near." Matt 4:17

Messianic Temptations and the Call of Disciples

MATTHEW 4:1–25 [1]*Then Jesus was led up by the Spirit into the wilderness to be tempted by the devil.* [2]*He fasted forty days and forty nights, and afterwards he was famished.* [3]*The tempter came and said to him, "If you are the Son of God, command these stones to become loaves of bread."* [4]*But he answered, "It is written,*

'One does not live by bread alone,

but by every word that comes from the mouth of God.'"

[5]*Then the devil took him to the holy city and placed him on the pinnacle of the temple,* [6]*saying to him, "If you are the Son of God, throw yourself down; for it is written,*

'He will command his angels concerning you,'

and 'On their hands they will bear you up,

so that you will not dash your foot against a stone.'"

[7]*Jesus said to him, "Again it is written, 'Do not put the Lord your God to the test.'"*

[8]*Again, the devil took him to a very high mountain and showed him all the kingdoms of the world and their splendor;* [9]*and he said to him, "All these I will give you, if you will fall down and worship me."* [10]*Jesus said to him, "Away with you, Satan! for it is written,*

'Worship the Lord your God,
  and serve only him.'"
¹¹*Then the devil left him, and suddenly angels came and waited on him.*

¹²*Now when Jesus heard that John had been arrested, he withdrew to Galilee.* ¹³*He left Nazareth and made his home in Capernaum by the sea, in the territory of Zebulun and Naphtali,* ¹⁴*so that what had been spoken through the prophet Isaiah might be fulfilled:*

¹⁵*"Land of Zebulun, land of Naphtali,*
  on the road by the sea, across the Jordan, Galilee of the Gentiles—
¹⁶*the people who sat in darkness*
  have seen a great light,
and for those who sat in the region and shadow of death
  light has dawned."

¹⁷*From that time Jesus began to proclaim, "Repent, for the kingdom of heaven has come near."*

¹⁸*As he walked by the Sea of Galilee, he saw two brothers, Simon, who is called Peter, and Andrew his brother, casting a net into the sea—for they were fishermen.* ¹⁹*And he said to them, "Follow me, and I will make you fish for people."* ²⁰*Immediately they left their nets and followed him.* ²¹*As he went from there, he saw two other brothers, James son of Zebedee and his brother John, in the boat with their father Zebedee, mending their nets, and he called them.* ²²*Immediately they left the boat and their father, and followed him.*

²³*Jesus went throughout Galilee, teaching in their synagogues and proclaiming the good news of the kingdom and curing every disease and every sickness among the people.* ²⁴*So his fame spread throughout all Syria, and they brought to him all the sick, those who were afflicted with various diseases and pains, demoniacs, epileptics, and paralytics, and he cured them.* ²⁵*And great crowds followed him from Galilee, the Decapolis, Jerusalem, Judea, and from beyond the Jordan.*

J esus' trial in the desert echoes Israel's forty-year sojourn in the desert following the exodus from Egypt. The scene takes its inspiration from Deuteronomy 6–8 in which Moses reviews the testing of God's people before their entry into the promised land. Moses calls this period to mind: "Remember the long way that the Lord your God has led you these forty years in the wilderness, in order to humble you, testing you to know what was in your heart" (Deut 8:3). The three replies given by Jesus in response to his testing are quotations from these chapters of Deuteronomy. Unlike Israel, which showed itself unfaithful in time of trial, Jesus remains steadfastly faithful to God's word.

Jesus is the Son of God who has been called out of Egypt (2:15). The tests given to Jesus by the devil challenge his identity as God's Son: "If you are the Son of God…" (verses 3, 6). Each of Jesus' responses indicates that he will not use his identity as Son of God for his own selfish ends. As the tests intensify, from the first exchange in the wilderness, then to the pinnacle of the temple, and finally to a high mountain, Jesus shows himself to be a model of covenant fidelity. He emerges from the desert as God's faithful and obedient Son.

For disciples of Jesus in the church to which Matthew wrote his gospel, each of Jesus' temptations is a challenge to examine their own responses. Each is a test that goes to the heart of what it means to be faithfully centered on God's covenant and to be a follower of his beloved Son. As Jesus was tested, so will the church be tested. But Matthew adds a note of comfort at the end of the wilderness account: When the devil left Jesus, angels came and waited on him. This ministration of angels assures disciples of God's protective care, no matter how intense the trials they face.

As Jesus begins his public ministry, he bases his work in Capernaum, a fishing village on the Sea of Galilee (verse 13). The prophetic citation from Isaiah 9:1–2 evokes Israel's hopes for restoration. The region of Galilee, seemingly a mixed population of Jews and Gentiles, was looked down upon by the religious establishment of Jerusalem. But into this place, waiting "in darkness" and in the "shadow of death," Jesus brings the "light" of the kingdom of God (verse 16). In him, God has come near his people and God's reign is immediately experienced.

The first disciples Jesus calls to share his mission are simple fishermen, not the religious elite whom one might expect for a spiritual mission. His invitation is simple: "Follow me" (verse 19). Normally in Jewish circles, disciples would search out a teacher. But Jesus takes the initiative and summons those he has chosen. The fishermen abandon their nets but they will still be fishing, casting a different kind of net by their own teaching and preaching. The disciples of the gospel form a bridge between the ministry of Jesus and the disciples who form the church to which Matthew addresses his gospel.

Reflection and Discussion

• What indicates that Jesus faced temptations throughout his life (see Matt 27:40; Heb 4:15)? What might have been his greatest test?

• What are the temptations that most test my identity as a son or daughter of God? What is the test I most often fail? What test proves my fidelity?

• How do I respond to the invitation of Jesus today to "Follow me"? In what ways do I share in his mission?

Prayer

Jesus, you walked the shores of the Sea of Galilee and chose people to follow you. Walk into my life today, call me by name, and give me a mission to serve your kingdom.

SUGGESTIONS FOR GROUP SESSION 2

1. If there are newcomers who were not present for the first group session, introduce them now.

2. You may want to pray this prayer as a group:

God of the past, present, and future, you work in every age to draw your people into your kingdom. Through the history of your people Israel, you prepared for the royal but humble birth of your Messiah. Through the preaching of John the Baptist and through testing in the wilderness, you prepared the way for the public ministry of your Son. As Jesus calls people into the community of disciples, help us to follow him, listen to his teaching, and always seek your kingdom.

3. Ask one or more of the following questions:
  • What was your biggest challenge in Bible study over this past week?
  • What did you learn about yourself this week?

4. Discuss lessons 1 through 6 together. Assuming that group members have read the Scripture and commentary during the week, there is no need to read it aloud. As you review each lesson, you might want to briefly summarize the Scripture passages of each lesson and ask the group what stands out most clearly from the commentary.

5. Choose one or more of the questions for reflection and discussion from each lesson to talk over as a group. You may want to ask group members which question was most challenging or helpful to them as you review each lesson.

6. Keep the discussion moving, but don't rush the discussion in order to complete more questions. Allow time for the questions that provoke the most discussion.

7. Instruct group members to complete lessons 7 through 12 on their own during the six days before the next group meeting. They should write out their own answers to the questions as preparation for next week's group discussion.

8. Conclude by praying aloud together the prayer at the end of lesson 6, or any other prayer you choose.

Let your light shine before others, so that they may see your good works and give glory to your Father in heaven. Matt 5:16

Discourse on the Mountain

MATTHEW 5:1–16 ¹*When Jesus saw the crowds, he went up the mountain; and after he sat down, his disciples came to him.* ²*Then he began to speak, and taught them, saying:*

³*"Blessed are the poor in spirit, for theirs is the kingdom of heaven.*

⁴*"Blessed are those who mourn, for they will be comforted.*

⁵*"Blessed are the meek, for they will inherit the earth.*

⁶*"Blessed are those who hunger and thirst for righteousness, for they will be filled.*

⁷*"Blessed are the merciful, for they will receive mercy.*

⁸*"Blessed are the pure in heart, for they will see God.*

⁹*"Blessed are the peacemakers, for they will be called children of God.*

¹⁰*"Blessed are those who are persecuted for righteousness' sake, for theirs is the kingdom of heaven.*

¹¹*"Blessed are you when people revile you and persecute you and utter all kinds of evil against you falsely on my account.* ¹²*Rejoice and be glad, for your reward is great in heaven, for in the same way they persecuted the prophets who were before you.*

¹³*"You are the salt of the earth; but if salt has lost its taste, how can its saltiness be restored? It is no longer good for anything, but is thrown out and trampled under foot.*

¹⁴*"You are the light of the world. A city built on a hill cannot be hid.* ¹⁵*No one after lighting a lamp puts it under the bushel basket, but on the lampstand, and it gives light to all in the house.* ¹⁶*In the same way, let your light shine before others, so that they may see your good works and give glory to your Father in heaven."*

Like Moses, Jesus has been rescued from death during his infancy, come out of Egypt, and been tested in the desert. Now, like Moses on Mount Sinai, Jesus ascends the mountain and from there teaches God's law (verse 1). This Sermon on the Mount is immediately addressed to the crowd that has gathered at the mountain. But like the Torah of Israel, the teaching of Jesus is also addressed to God's people of all times. Jesus has proclaimed that the kingdom of heaven has come near. Now, in this great sermon, Jesus begins to teach what life under the reign of God is like.

The eight beatitudes name the key character traits of those who are blessed by God. These eight characteristics are evidence of God's gracious gifts offered to those who repent at the message of the kingdom. The beatitudes are divided into two sets of four: first, those qualities that describe our relationship to God (verses 3–6), then, those qualities that describe our relationship with other people (verses 7–10). These gifts offered to the repentant must be cultivated in the lifelong process of discipleship so that they become more dynamically present. Each of these eight characteristics of blessedness is followed by the promises of God. The present experience of God's reign in Jesus motivates the disciple to live in hopeful confidence of its future intensification.

The "poor in spirit" are those who admit their poverty and acknowledge their total dependence on God. Those who cultivate this trust in God will begin experiencing the kingdom in their present lives and await its full realization. "Those who mourn" are those who lament their own sins as well as the sin of the world. The mourning that results from afflictions and persecution will be met with God's future comfort. The "meek" are those who possess an unassuming humility, based on the model of Jesus. The earth will ultimately be inherited by these, rather than by those stocked with wealth, status, and arms. "Those who hunger and thirst for righteousness" realize their lack of right behavior before God and desire that righteousness permeate society and culture. This deep desire for God's will to be done on earth will be satisfied with the full coming of God's kingdom.

Those who are "merciful" in relationship to other people demonstrate compassion and loving kindness modeled on the life and teachings of Jesus. Those who deal mercifully with others will receive God's ultimate mercy and obtain the promises of his faithful love. Those who are "pure in heart" possess an internal integrity and single-heartedness which manifests itself in both their private and public lives. The "peacemakers" are those who actively seek harmonious relationships with others. Their experience of peace with God enables them to strive for the cessation of hostilities and active reconciliation between people, while awaiting God's ultimate peace to come upon the world. Persecution "for righteousness' sake" is what those seeking to live the values taught by Jesus can expect to experience, but the second assurance of "the kingdom of heaven" brings the beatitudes full circle (verses 3, 10).

The lives of those living under God's reign are marked by humility toward God and mercy toward others. Though we might expect such humble, merciful people to be valued by other people, such is not the case for most disciples of Jesus. Scorn, insult, and abuse are what followers of Jesus more often receive in the present age (verses 11–12). Though this assurance of blessedness might seem to be an additional beatitude, it is more of an expansion of the others. Those who receive harassment and maltreatment must not simply endure it, but experience it with deep joy, knowing that they are following in the way of the prophets before them and identifying themselves with Jesus, who was persecuted to the point of death. These countercultural blessings of the beatitudes mark Christians as out of step with the world and as witnesses to God's kingdom.

As Christians bear witness by living out the beatitudes they become "the salt of the earth" and "the light of the world" (verses 13–16). Their mission has a wide horizon, far beyond the narrow circle of the disciples themselves. Like salt, they bring zest to the world and bring out the best in others. As light in the world, they are a flame of faith and a beacon of hope. Without visible works, a disciple is of no more value than tasteless salt or a lamp under a basket. Authentic disciples affect people through the character traits named in the beatitudes, and as people see their good works, they give glory to God.

Reflection and Discussion

• How can I be "poor in spirit" while living in the midst of material prosperity?

• Through which of the beatitudes is Jesus speaking most directly to me today?

• How am I like salt and light for others? How can I be a clearer witness of God's presence in the world?

Prayer

Divine Teacher, you guide your disciples to understand the ways of God's kingdom. I believe that you want to bring blessings to my life as I follow your way. Transform me into the kind of person described by the beatitudes.

"Do not think that I have come to abolish the law or the prophets; I have come not to abolish but to fulfill." Matt 5:17

Ethics of the Kingdom

MATTHEW 5:17–37 [17]*"Do not think that I have come to abolish the law or the prophets; I have come not to abolish but to fulfill.* [18]*For truly I tell you, until heaven and earth pass away, not one letter, not one stroke of a letter, will pass from the law until all is accomplished.* [19]*Therefore, whoever breaks one of the least of these commandments, and teaches others to do the same, will be called least in the kingdom of heaven; but whoever does them and teaches them will be called great in the kingdom of heaven.* [20]*For I tell you, unless your righteousness exceeds that of the scribes and Pharisees, you will never enter the kingdom of heaven.*

[21]*"You have heard that it was said to those of ancient times, 'You shall not murder'; and 'whoever murders shall be liable to judgment.'* [22]*But I say to you that if you are angry with a brother or sister, you will be liable to judgment; and if you insult a brother or sister, you will be liable to the council; and if you say, 'You fool,' you will be liable to the hell of fire.* [23]*So when you are offering your gift at the altar, if you remember that your brother or sister has something against you,* [24]*leave your gift there before the altar and go; first be reconciled to your brother or sister, and then come and offer your gift.* [25]*Come to terms quickly with your accuser while you are on the way to court with him, or your accuser may hand you over to the judge, and the judge to the guard, and you will be thrown into prison.* [26]*Truly I tell you, you will never get out until you have paid the last penny.*

[27]*"You have heard that it was said, 'You shall not commit adultery.'* [28]*But I say*

38

to you that everyone who looks at a woman with lust has already committed adultery with her in his heart. ²⁹If your right eye causes you to sin, tear it out and throw it away; it is better for you to lose one of your members than for your whole body to be thrown into hell. ³⁰And if your right hand causes you to sin, cut it off and throw it away; it is better for you to lose one of your members than for your whole body to go into hell.

³¹"It was also said, 'Whoever divorces his wife, let him give her a certificate of divorce.' ³²But I say to you that anyone who divorces his wife, except on the ground of unchastity, causes her to commit adultery; and whoever marries a divorced woman commits adultery.

³³"Again, you have heard that it was said to those of ancient times, 'You shall not swear falsely, but carry out the vows you have made to the Lord.' ³⁴But I say to you, Do not swear at all, either by heaven, for it is the throne of God, ³⁵or by the earth, for it is his footstool, or by Jerusalem, for it is the city of the great King. ³⁶And do not swear by your head, for you cannot make one hair white or black. ³⁷Let your word be 'Yes, Yes' or 'No, No'; anything more than this comes from the evil one."

Jesus states that he has not come to abolish or invalidate "the law or the prophets," the Jewish terminology for the ancient Scriptures. In fact, these Scriptures are so permanent that not even the smallest letter or stroke of the pen will be done away with until the end of the world (verse 18). Jesus is a thoroughly observant Jew who is devoted to following in the way of the Torah, demonstrating his belief in the eternal validity of the ancient Scriptures.

Yet, the teaching of Jesus is not simply a restatement of the precepts contained in the Old Testament. His mission is to "fulfill" the Torah, the covenant, and the prophets of old (verse 18). This means that he brings the Hebrew Scriptures to their divinely intended goal, because they point to him. Since Jesus is the Messiah, the end or goal of the ancient Scriptures, he is the authoritative, definitive interpreter of the law for the messianic age. His life and teaching fulfill the Torah, revealing its ultimate meaning and accomplishing its purpose.

By the time of Jesus, the Torah of Israel had been subjected to centuries of interpretive tradition, and many differing interpretations of various parts of the law were followed by the Jewish people. Jesus does not contradict anything in the Hebrew Bible, but his teachings are new in the sense that they transcend the established understanding of the law promulgated by the religious leaders. His disciples, then, must obey him, as the law's ultimate interpreter, and teach his interpretation in order to be fit for the kingdom of heaven (verse 19).

Jesus then expands the general statement of his relationship to the law into a series of specific teachings that illustrate what it means to "fulfill" the law. Each of these illustrations is introduced by the phrase "you have heard that it was said..." and followed by Jesus' own authoritative teaching, "but I say to you..." These teachings of Jesus do not contradict the Torah, but rather they clarify its deepest meaning and restore its original divine intention. Each illustration calls for a more challenging and thorough fidelity to the law on the level of both external actions and internal disposition.

In the first illustration, Jesus teaches that the prohibition of murder implicitly prohibits the anger and abusive speech that can lead to violence (verses 21–22). In contrast to such heated rage and verbal abuse, the disciple should always seek to initiate reconciliation. Offering concrete examples, Jesus says that fellow disciples should seek reconciliation over any offense before bringing a sacrifice to be offered in the temple (verses 23–24). He also teaches that adversaries should seek reconciliation out of court rather than suffer the dire consequences of judicial punishment (verse 25). Jesus' teaching shows how the heart of the law is aimed at broken relationships that need to be healed.

The second illustration demonstrates that the law against adultery implicitly prohibits lust (verses 27–28). Jesus again shows the close relationship of external actions and internal dispositions. Lustful desires and coveting the spouse of another are ways of committing adultery in the heart. Jesus' hyperboles do not advocate bodily dismemberment, but stress the importance of doing whatever is necessary to control the natural passions that tend to flare out of control. Jesus extends his teaching on adultery to demonstrate how divorce can also lead to adultery (verses 31–32). He contradicts the permissive interpretation of many Jewish teachers who listed numerous reasons for allowing divorce. Jesus' authoritative teaching is rooted in God's original intent for marriage as a permanent and inviolable union.

The next illustration addresses honesty in relationships. Though the Torah forbids swearing an oath falsely, Jesus teaches that a disciple's word alone ought to be reliable without being supported by an oath. As in all the other illustrations, it is the content of one's heart that matters most, both in relationship with God and with other people.

Reflection and Discussion

• How does Jesus show that fidelity to God's law goes beyond the literal requirements of the law?

• Does my external obedience to God's law reflect my internal attitude? How might God wish to change my heart?

• Which of Jesus' illustrations of the law's fulfillment is most challenging to me? How would a more faithful response to this teaching change my life?

Prayer

Lord Jesus, you invoke the law of Moses and teach God's law with authority. Help me to understand your teachings and live in a way that marks me as your disciple. May the actions of my life proclaim the presence of your kingdom.

But I say to you, Love your enemies and pray for those who persecute you, so that you may be children of your Father in heaven. Matt 5:44–45

The Principle of Radical Love

MATTHEW 5:38–48 [38]*"You have heard that it was said, 'An eye for an eye and a tooth for a tooth.'* [39]*But I say to you, Do not resist an evildoer. But if anyone strikes you on the right cheek, turn the other also;* [40]*and if anyone wants to sue you and take your coat, give your cloak as well;* [41]*and if anyone forces you to go one mile, go also the second mile.* [42]*Give to everyone who begs from you, and do not refuse anyone who wants to borrow from you.*

[43]*"You have heard that it was said, 'You shall love your neighbor and hate your enemy.'* [44]*But I say to you, Love your enemies and pray for those who persecute you,* [45]*so that you may be children of your Father in heaven; for he makes his sun rise on the evil and on the good, and sends rain on the righteous and on the unrighteous.* [46]*For if you love those who love you, what reward do you have? Do not even the tax collectors do the same?* [47]*And if you greet only your brothers and sisters, what more are you doing than others? Do not even the Gentiles do the same?* [48]*Be perfect, therefore, as your heavenly Father is perfect."*

Jesus continues to offer illustrations of how his teaching fulfils the Torah of Israel, clarifying its deepest meaning and restoring its original divine intention. In this illustration, Jesus first restates the biblical principle of retaliation in kind as found in Exodus, Leviticus, and Deuteronomy (verse 38). This commandment insists that the punishment should match the offense, thus preventing escalating cycles of revenge. Then Jesus insists that disciples should abandon the idea of retribution altogether and not retaliate against an evil person (verse 39).

The examples offered by Jesus teach disciples not to passively submit to injustice, but to respond in a creative, nonviolent way. When insulted with a backhanded slap on the cheek, the disciple should turn and offer the other cheek as well. This shames the aggressor and robs the antagonist of the power to humiliate. When a debtor is forced to give his inner garment as collateral or to repay a debt, he should give his outer garment as well. When the debtor stands naked in court, he performs a shocking act that shames the creditor, exposing the injustices of the financial system. When a Roman soldier conscripts a disciple to carry his equipment for a mile, he should carry it for two miles. In this way, the disciple seizes the initiative and the soldier risks punishment for demanding excessive service from the occupied population. In all of these examples, Jesus encourages his followers to respond with disproportionate kindness, promoting the good with a generous, benevolent response. This kind of response interrupts a cycle of violent revenge in a creative way, nudging the aggressor toward repentance and a cycle of generosity.

Jesus' final illustration, and the principle on which all the others are based, is his teaching on love. The command to "love your neighbor" (Lev 19:18) is found in the Torah, but nowhere in the Old Testament is there a command to hate your enemy (verse 43). It was generally understood, however, that such love was required toward those who shared in Israel's covenant but not necessarily toward those outside the community. For Jesus, love even for enemies gets at the heart of the commandment's divine intent and goal. His teachings always transcend typical human practice and call his disciples to love without boundaries.

In the examples Jesus offers, he demonstrates that love concerns not just emotions but actions. Praying for your persecutors is a striking demonstration of love for them (verse 44). Welcoming outsiders who are not part of your community is another ways of putting the commandment to love into practice in a manner that transcends cultural norms (verse 47). The motivation for all these loving actions is not just to receive reciprocal treatment, but rather to imitate the way God loves. Disciples are to model in their lives the universal benevolence of the Father (verse 45).

Jesus' final exhortation sums up all that Jesus has taught so far in his Sermon on the Mount. By seeking to fulfill the law, practicing the commands of the Torah in a way that expresses their fullest goal and God's complete intention, we become "perfect" as God is perfect (verse 48). The Greek term does not suggest static flawlessness, as the term can imply in English. It means, rather, "whole" or "complete." It is an invitation to begin living in God's reign, reaching always toward the fullness of the future kingdom that God has promised. By loving as God loves, disciples model God's very character and become salt and light in the world.

Reflection and Discussion

• Are Jesus' teachings against retaliation and on love of enemies realistic today?

• What might be an example of a creative, nonviolent way I might respond to someone who seeks to insult or do harm to me?

• In what ways do the teachings of Jesus differ from passivity in the face of injustice?

• What are some ways in which Jesus' teachings on active nonviolence have been implemented in communities and nations in recent decades?

• What are the limits of my love for others? How does Jesus challenge me to expand the range of my love?

Prayer

Good Teacher, you call your disciples to transcend the common and accepted responses of our society. I realize that if my life is just like everyone else's, no one will recognize that I am your disciple. Help me to set myself apart by the completeness of my love.

Our Father in heaven, hallowed be your name. Your kingdom come. Your will be done, on earth as it is in heaven. Matt 6:9–10

Spiritual Practices within the Kingdom

MATTHEW 6:1–23 [1]*"Beware of practicing your piety before others in order to be seen by them; for then you have no reward from your Father in heaven.*

[2]*"So whenever you give alms, do not sound a trumpet before you, as the hypocrites do in the synagogues and in the streets, so that they may be praised by others. Truly I tell you, they have received their reward.* [3]*But when you give alms, do not let your left hand know what your right hand is doing,* [4]*so that your alms may be done in secret; and your Father who sees in secret will reward you.*

[5]*"And whenever you pray, do not be like the hypocrites; for they love to stand and pray in the synagogues and at the street corners, so that they may be seen by others. Truly I tell you, they have received their reward.* [6]*But whenever you pray, go into your room and shut the door and pray to your Father who is in secret; and your Father who sees in secret will reward you.*

[7]*"When you are praying, do not heap up empty phrases as the Gentiles do; for they think that they will be heard because of their many words.* [8]*Do not be like them, for your Father knows what you need before you ask him.*

[9]*"Pray then in this way:*

Our Father in heaven,

hallowed be your name.
[10]Your kingdom come.
Your will be done,
* on earth as it is in heaven.*
[11]Give us this day our daily bread.
[12]And forgive us our debts,
* as we also have forgiven our debtors.*
[13]And do not bring us to the time of trial,
* but rescue us from the evil one.*

[14]For if you forgive others their trespasses, your heavenly Father will also forgive you; [15]but if you do not forgive others, neither will your Father forgive your trespasses.

[16]"And whenever you fast, do not look dismal, like the hypocrites, for they disfigure their faces so as to show others that they are fasting. Truly I tell you, they have received their reward. [17]But when you fast, put oil on your head and wash your face, [18]so that your fasting may be seen not by others but by your Father who is in secret; and your Father who sees in secret will reward you.

[19]"Do not store up for yourselves treasures on earth, where moth and rust consume and where thieves break in and steal; [20]but store up for yourselves treasures in heaven, where neither moth nor rust consumes and where thieves do not break in and steal. [21]For where your treasure is, there your heart will be also.

[22]"The eye is the lamp of the body. So, if your eye is healthy, your whole body will be full of light; [23]but if your eye is unhealthy, your whole body will be full of darkness. If then the light in you is darkness, how great is the darkness!"

This section of the Sermon on the Mount focuses on three traditional acts of Jewish piety: almsgiving (verses 1–4), prayer (verses 5–15), and fasting (verses 16–18). Jesus does not criticize the practices themselves; rather, as in his previous teachings on the Torah, he challenges his hearers to probe the deepest reasons for the acts and to consider the internal dispositions from which the external practices arise. He criticizes the ostentatious display of almsgiving, prayer, and fasting. Public recognition is the only reward for those who perform their religious actions in order to be seen (verses 2, 5, 16). God rewards those who keep their actions private (verses 4, 6, 18). What is emphasized here is not really favoring private over public forms of spiritual practices but the guiding intention and inner spirit of all religious acts.

The Lord's Prayer is the center of this section and describes the inner attitudes that motivate the true disciple. Jesus prefaces this prayer with the remark that the Father knows what we need before we ask (verse 8). Still, Jesus teaches us to pray. In addressing the prayer to "our Father," Jesus demonstrates his desire to share his personal relationship with God as Father with us (verse 9). It is a prayer that comes from the heart of Jesus. Though it has become through the centuries the hallmark of Christian prayer, it is thoroughly Jewish. There is nothing in it that a Jew in the time of Jesus or today would not pray to God.

Prayer is not a one-way street and it does not require a multitude of words. This prayer of Jesus highlights the prayer of praise, contrition, and petition. It contains six petitions: the first three focus on God (verses 9–10) and the next three ask God to help us with our human needs for sustenance, forgiveness, and strength in the face of testing and evil (verses 11–13). The entire prayer anticipates the coming of God's kingdom, praying that God will bring about the fullness of the kingdom in the future, while we live in the present in accord with the vision of God's reign among us. The expectation of future fullness leads to present ethical imperatives. While we hope for the future kingdom, we pray for the practical and urgent needs we find as we live in a world not yet fully conformed to God's will.

Reflection and Discussion

• What is the common theme in Jesus' teachings on almsgiving, prayer, and fasting? In what way does it challenge me the most?

• What might be the purpose of praying, then, if God already knows our needs before we ask?

• What aspects of the Lord's Prayer do I notice when I imagine the prayer coming from the heart and lips of Jesus?

• What might Jesus mean when he teaches, "Where your treasure is, there your heart will be also"? How could almsgiving, prayer, or fasting help my heart to find its treasure?

Prayer

Lord Jesus, I don't want to be like the hypocrites, performing religious deeds while my heart is far away from God. Help me to develop a heart like your own and to pray in the way you taught me.

Strive first for the kingdom of God and his righteousness, and all these things will be given to you as well. Matt 6:33

Wealth, Anxiety, and Trust

MATTHEW 6:24–34 ²⁴*"No one can serve two masters; for a slave will either hate the one and love the other, or be devoted to the one and despise the other. You cannot serve God and wealth.*

²⁵*"Therefore I tell you, do not worry about your life, what you will eat or what you will drink, or about your body, what you will wear. Is not life more than food, and the body more than clothing?* ²⁶*Look at the birds of the air; they neither sow nor reap nor gather into barns, and yet your heavenly Father feeds them. Are you not of more value than they?* ²⁷*And can any of you by worrying add a single hour to your span of life?* ²⁸*And why do you worry about clothing? Consider the lilies of the field, how they grow; they neither toil nor spin,* ²⁹*yet I tell you, even Solomon in all his glory was not clothed like one of these.* ³⁰*But if God so clothes the grass of the field, which is alive today and tomorrow is thrown into the oven, will he not much more clothe you—you of little faith?* ³¹*Therefore do not worry, saying, 'What will we eat?' or 'What will we drink?' or 'What will we wear?'* ³²*For it is the Gentiles who strive for all these things; and indeed your heavenly Father knows that you need all these things.* ³³*But strive first for the kingdom of God and his righteousness, and all these things will be given to you as well.*

^{34}*"So do not worry about tomorrow, for tomorrow will bring worries of its own. Today's trouble is enough for today."*

Calling God "our Father" must surely mean that we can trust God. This section of Jesus' sermon shows us what it means to trust God in the way that we live. Trusting in wealth is a serious obstacle to trusting God. Jesus challenges us to question the priorities of our lives: Do we put God, or the wealth of this world, first in our lives? Just as a slave cannot adequately serve two masters, inevitably being devoted to one over the other, Jesus tells his disciples, "You cannot serve God and wealth" (verse 24). When we focus our priorities on God, our lives are ruled by his goodness and love. When we give earthly wealth our undivided attention, it becomes our master and we become its slaves.

Another obstacle to trusting God is worry. Jesus first offers a general command: "Do not worry about your life, what you will eat or what you will drink, or about your body, what you will wear" (verse 25). This kind of worry is not the ordinary concern we must have about life's necessities. Rather, it is undue anxiety that does not trust the Father's loving care. If we cannot serve both God and wealth, then we cannot be overly anxious about the things that wealth can provide. The command is followed by a rhetorical question asking whether life is not more than food and the body more than clothing. The response should be "of course," knowing that God who gives life will certainly supply the means to sustain it.

This is followed by Jesus' exhortation to observe the birds of the air (verse 26). They do not grow their food, let alone grow anxious about it, but the Father gives them all the food they need. This encouragement to reflect on God's providential care for the birds is followed by another rhetorical question. Jesus asks whether we are not more valuable than they. Knowing that we are made in God's image, surely God will provide for all that we need. A follow-up rhetorical question asks if we can add to our lifespan by worrying (verse 28). Of course we can't, and we know today that anxiety and stress will surely shorten the span of our lives.

Jesus' encouragement to observe the birds of the air is followed by his exhortation to consider the lilies of the field. He shifts the focus here from food to clothing. These flowers do not work to create their clothing, yet they are more wondrously dressed than King Solomon in all his royal splendor. The rhetorical question leads Jesus' listeners to reflect on God's wonderful providence. If God cares so much for plants, which have such a brief lifespan, surely God will provide the clothing we need for our bodies (verse 30). Hesitation to trust God for all of our needs is due to our "little faith." This gentle rebuke is directed to followers whose faith is real but faltering. It is Jesus' way of saying, "Trust in God. Don't let your worries keep you from believing that God will provide for you. Deepening your faith will provide you with a fuller life."

In essence, Jesus tells the crowds on the mountain and all his future disciples to put first things first: God's kingdom must be the primary concern of disciples (verse 33). Excessively worrying about the future only marginalizes God and the priorities of his kingdom from our lives. Tomorrow's food and clothing should not be our focus. Disciples must address themselves to the matters at hand today while trusting that tomorrow is in the hands of our loving Father. In this way the ordinary planning and work required for our daily needs will not be motivated by, or lead to, the anxiety that distracts from our allegiance to God's kingdom.

Reflection and Discussion

• What are the primary obstacles that prevent me from trusting adequately in God?

• What parts of my checking account or charge card would suggest an anxious concern over what I will eat and what I will wear? What parts of my finances reveal the priorities of God's kingdom?

• What are the issues about which I worry excessively?

• How does reflecting on the birds of the air and the lilies of the field help me to worry less and trust more?

• What does Jesus mean by his teaching, "Strive first for the kingdom of God" (verse 33)? How can I practice this teaching each day?

Prayer

Jesus, our Father keeps the birds and the flowers in existence and provides for their daily needs. Free me from needless anxiety as I seek to make my first priority the concerns of your kingdom and the things that last forever.

"Everyone then who hears these words of mine and acts on them will be like a wise man who built his house on rock." Matt 7:24

Wisdom under God's Reign

MATTHEW 7:1–29 ¹*"Do not judge, so that you may not be judged. ²For with the judgment you make you will be judged, and the measure you give will be the measure you get. ³Why do you see the speck in your neighbor's eye, but do not notice the log in your own eye? ⁴Or how can you say to your neighbor, 'Let me take the speck out of your eye,' while the log is in your own eye? ⁵You hypocrite, first take the log out of your own eye, and then you will see clearly to take the speck out of your neighbor's eye.*

⁶*"Do not give what is holy to dogs; and do not throw your pearls before swine, or they will trample them under foot and turn and maul you.*

⁷*"Ask, and it will be given you; search, and you will find; knock, and the door will be opened for you. ⁸For everyone who asks receives, and everyone who searches finds, and for everyone who knocks, the door will be opened. ⁹Is there anyone among you who, if your child asks for bread, will give a stone? ¹⁰Or if the child asks for a fish, will give a snake? ¹¹If you then, who are evil, know how to give good gifts to your children, how much more will your Father in heaven give good things to those who ask him!*

¹²*"In everything do to others as you would have them do to you; for this is the law and the prophets.*

¹³*"Enter through the narrow gate; for the gate is wide and the road is easy that leads to destruction, and there are many who take it. ¹⁴For the gate is narrow*

and the road is hard that leads to life, and there are few who find it.

¹⁵*"Beware of false prophets, who come to you in sheep's clothing but inwardly are ravenous wolves.* ¹⁶*You will know them by their fruits. Are grapes gathered from thorns, or figs from thistles?* ¹⁷*In the same way, every good tree bears good fruit, but the bad tree bears bad fruit.* ¹⁸*A good tree cannot bear bad fruit, nor can a bad tree bear good fruit.* ¹⁹*Every tree that does not bear good fruit is cut down and thrown into the fire.* ²⁰*Thus you will know them by their fruits.*

²¹*"Not everyone who says to me, 'Lord, Lord,' will enter the kingdom of heaven, but only the one who does the will of my Father in heaven.* ²²*On that day many will say to me, 'Lord, Lord, did we not prophesy in your name, and cast out demons in your name, and do many deeds of power in your name?'* ²³*Then I will declare to them, 'I never knew you; go away from me, you evildoers.'*

²⁴*"Everyone then who hears these words of mine and acts on them will be like a wise man who built his house on rock.* ²⁵*The rain fell, the floods came, and the winds blew and beat on that house, but it did not fall, because it had been founded on rock.* ²⁶*And everyone who hears these words of mine and does not act on them will be like a foolish man who built his house on sand.* ²⁷*The rain fell, and the floods came, and the winds blew and beat against that house, and it fell—and great was its fall!"*

²⁸*Now when Jesus had finished saying these things, the crowds were astounded at his teaching,* ²⁹*for he taught them as one having authority, and not as their scribes.*

These teachings of Jesus take the form of sayings, illustrations, commands, and reflections, strung together like pearls on a string. They are put together like the wisdom writings of the Old Testament (Proverbs, Ecclesiastes, and Sirach). First, Jesus forbids an overcritical judgmentalism that scrutinizes others without even glancing at ourselves. Jesus commands us to look honestly at ourselves before we attempt the delicate task of judging others. His vivid metaphors of the log and the speck communicate his message in a dramatic and memorable way.

Jesus' next warning about not giving what is valuable and holy to dogs and swine is the opposite of his previous teaching. We must not be judgmental, but neither can we be oblivious to those who seek to do evil. The priceless and sacred message of the kingdom must be treated with discernment, since malicious people will seek to bring harm and destruction to God's reign. When we remove the log from our eye, we will be able to discern the difference between being judgmental toward those with a relatively minor problem and naïve toward those who seek to do great harm.

Jesus again presents God as a loving Father who desires to give good things to his children (verses 7–11). Rhetorical questions emphasize the wise parental qualities of God. Like parents who have almost limitless concern for their children, God cares for us so intimately that all we have to do is turn to him with our needs. When we ask, seek, and knock, we can be confident that our God will respond in the way that he knows best.

The essence of biblical ethics, Jesus summarizes, is found in the maxim: Treat other people just as you would like to be treated by them (verse 12). Similar teachings are found in other Jewish literature, and the Torah offers a similar command: "You shall love your neighbor as yourself" (Lev 19:18). A negative form of the saying is found in the writings: "What you hate, do not do to anyone" (Tob 4:15). The teaching seems simple, but it offers us a challenging standard for our daily choices.

The Sermon on the Mount concludes with a series of exhortations to put Jesus' teachings into practice. Each contrasts two ways of life that require a choice. This option of the two ways is rooted in Deuteronomy. Here God offers Israel a choice between a blessing and a curse, between life and death, between prosperity and adversity (Deut 11:26; 30:15). Jesus contrasts the wide gate and the easy road that leads to destruction with the narrow gate and the difficult road that leads to life (verses 13–14). Jesus urges us to choose to enter the narrow gate and to take the rugged road, metaphors for repentance and the life of Christian discipleship. Jesus then contrasts true teachers and false prophets, which are like good trees and bad trees (verses 15–20). We can discern the difference between them by examining their results, the good or bad fruit that they produce. Finally Jesus contrasts the one who builds his house on rock and the one who builds on sand. The house built on solid bedrock withstands the storms and floods and does not collapse, while the house built on shifting sand is destroyed.

In all of these contrasting metaphors, the key to success is choosing to act on the words of Jesus. Wise disciples act on what they hear from their master; foolish people complacently hear and do nothing. Jesus warns that entrance into the kingdom is not guaranteed because we have listened and know the right words. Saying "Lord, Lord," either in addressing Jesus or professing belief, will not assure us of salvation (verse 21). It is our actions, doing the will of God, which will allow us to enter God's reign.

Reflection and Discussion

• Jesus is using humorous imagery when he suggests that we take the log out of our own eye before we concern ourselves with the speck in our neighbor's eye. Why is this kind of exaggerated and playful imagery effective when teaching others?

• When have I been disappointed in another because their actions did not match their words? Which of my words or actions could use a change?

• On what bedrock do I wish to build my life? What words of Jesus' sermon do I want to put into action today?

Prayer

Merciful Judge, you alone know my heart and the heart of others. Teach me to follow the way that leads to life in your kingdom. Guide my choices so that I will build my life on the solid foundation of your teachings.

SUGGESTIONS FOR FACILITATORS, GROUP SESSION 3

1. Welcome group members and ask if there are any announcements anyone would like to make.

2. You may want to pray this prayer as a group:

Saving God, you have given your church the sermon of Jesus offered on the mountain, and you have commanded us to listen to him. Encourage us to take these teachings to heart and help us to live in a way that identifies us as disciples of Jesus. Guide our choices, free us from needless anxiety, and help us to make your kingdom our first priority. As we study your sacred Scriptures, encourage us and guide us with the inspiration of your Holy Spirit.

3. Ask one or more of the following questions:
   • Which image from the lessons this week stands out most memorably to you?
   • What is the most important lesson you learned through your study this week?

4. Discuss lessons 7 through 12. Choose one or more of the questions for reflection and discussion from each lesson to discuss as a group. You may want to ask group members which question was most challenging or helpful to them as you review each lesson.

5. Remember that there are no definitive answers for these discussion questions. The insights of group members will add to the understanding of all. None of these questions require an expert.

6. After talking about each lesson, instruct group members to complete lessons 13 through 18 on their own during the six days before the next group meeting. They should write out their own answers to the questions as preparation for next week's group discussion.

7. Ask the group if anyone is having any particular problems with the Bible study during the week. You may want to share advice and encouragement within the group.

8. Conclude by praying aloud together the prayer at the end of one of the lessons discussed. You may add to the prayer based on the sharing that has occurred in the group.

**"Lord, I am not worthy to have you come under my roof;
but only speak the word, and my servant will be healed."** Matt 8:8

The Messiah's Healing Work

MATTHEW 8:1–17 ¹*When Jesus had come down from the mountain, great crowds followed him;* ²*and there was a leper who came to him and knelt before him, saying, "Lord, if you choose, you can make me clean."* ³*He stretched out his hand and touched him, saying, "I do choose. Be made clean!" Immediately his leprosy was cleansed.* ⁴*Then Jesus said to him, "See that you say nothing to anyone; but go, show yourself to the priest, and offer the gift that Moses commanded, as a testimony to them."*

⁵*When he entered Capernaum, a centurion came to him, appealing to him* ⁶*and saying, "Lord, my servant is lying at home paralyzed, in terrible distress."* ⁷*And he said to him, "I will come and cure him."* ⁸*The centurion answered, "Lord, I am not worthy to have you come under my roof; but only speak the word, and my servant will be healed.* ⁹*For I also am a man under authority, with soldiers under me; and I say to one, 'Go,' and he goes, and to another, 'Come,' and he comes, and to my slave, 'Do this,' and the slave does it."* ¹⁰*When Jesus heard him, he was amazed and said to those who followed him, "Truly I tell you, in no one in Israel have I found such faith.* ¹¹*I tell you, many will come from east and west and will eat with Abraham and Isaac and Jacob in the kingdom of heaven,* ¹²*while the heirs of the kingdom will be thrown into the outer darkness,*

where there will be weeping and gnashing of teeth." [13]*And to the centurion Jesus said, "Go; let it be done for you according to your faith." And the servant was healed in that hour.*

[14]*When Jesus entered Peter's house, he saw his mother-in-law lying in bed with a fever;* [15]*he touched her hand, and the fever left her, and she got up and began to serve him.* [16]*That evening they brought to him many who were possessed with demons; and he cast out the spirits with a word, and cured all who were sick.* [17]*This was to fulfill what had been spoken through the prophet Isaiah, "He took our infirmities and bore our diseases."*

A s the Sermon on the Mount offers Jesus' authoritative teaching, this section of the gospel displays his authoritative healing. In these first three accounts, Jesus heals a leper, the servant of a centurion, and Peter's mother-in-law. Each of these was powerless and marginalized in Jewish society. The leper was an outcast from all social and religious functions. The Roman centurion was a Gentile with no religious status. As a woman, Peter's mother-in-law was excluded from many privileges available only to men. Yet Jesus crossed the boundaries: he touched the leper, praised the faith of the Gentile, and anticipated the woman's need and healed her before any request to do so. Through these healings, Jesus demonstrates that qualms about ritual purity, ethnic exclusivism, and gender stereotypes do not hinder his mission. It is just these people from the margins of society who are most receptive to the message of the kingdom.

Because of leprosy's contagion and its revolting visible impact, lepers were banned from social contact. Yet the leper shows courage even in approaching Jesus. He kneels in front of Jesus and addresses him as "Lord" (verse 2). Jesus bridges the remaining distance between them by reaching out his hand and touching the leper. The touch of Jesus immediately heals him of leprosy, and his skin is cleansed. Jesus then directs the man to follow the steps specified by the Torah (Lev 14). He must be certified as cleansed by a priest and offer sacrifices at the temple in order to be readmitted to society. Again Jesus demonstrates that he has come not to abolish the law of Moses but to fulfill it.

The centurion is a Roman army commander. He approaches Jesus and tells him that his servant is bedridden with severe pain and paralysis (verse 6). When Jesus offers to go to the centurion's home and cure his servant, the officer professes his unworthiness and acknowledges his belief that Jesus can heal his servant with only a word. The centurion knows that just as he is authorized to command soldiers and count on their obedience, Jesus has the same power over illness and evil. Jesus then uses the confidence of this non-Jewish officer as an opportunity to teach his disciples. Praising the faith of this Gentile, Jesus recalls the words of the prophets who looked forward to the day when Gentiles would come from throughout the world to feast with Israel's ancestors at the banquet of God's kingdom (verse 11). Because of the centurion's great faith, Jesus heals his servant, not with a touch, but with only a word and at a distance. The centurion is a forerunner of the many Gentiles who will be called to the kingdom through Christ's church. Both Jewish Christians and Gentile Christians will be able to look back at the trusting confidence of the centurion as a model for their faith.

The third account is the healing of Peter's mother-in-law. Unlike the other healing accounts, in which people come to Jesus to request a cure, here Jesus takes the initiative. Coming into Peter's house, Jesus sees her need, touches her hand, and the fever leaves her (verses 14–15). The immediacy and totality of her healing underlines the authority of Jesus, and her reaction indicates the ideal response in service to Jesus.

Again Matthew adds a quotation from the Scriptures to indicate the deeper significance of Jesus' acts. The fulfillment passage is from Isaiah's description of the Suffering Servant: "He took our infirmities and bore our diseases." (Isa 53:4). The gospel here links Jesus' redemptive suffering and death with his healing of sickness and diseases. The individual instances of healing during Jesus' ministry, though only temporary, anticipate the full redemption and complete human healing that we await with the full coming of God's kingdom.

Reflection and Discussion

• What do the type of people healed by Jesus in these accounts say about the scope of his mission?

• What is the role of faith in these healings? Do I have this kind of trusting confidence in Jesus?

• None of these three—the leper, the Gentile, or the woman—could enter the sacred area of the temple, where Jewish males presented their offerings to the priests. Why would Matthew choose to highlight Jesus' healing of these three?

• What insight do the final words from Isaiah give me about Jesus? In what sense is healing a part of Jesus' saving mission?

Prayer

Lord, I am not worthy that you should enter under my roof, but only say the word and my soul shall be healed. Give me the confidence of the leper to come to you in faith, and the trust of the centurion to believe in your healing power.

"What sort of man is this, that even the winds and the sea obey him?"
Matt 8:27

The Messiah Manifests Divine Power

MATTHEW 8:18–9:8 [18]*Now when Jesus saw great crowds around him, he gave orders to go over to the other side.* [19]*A scribe then approached and said, "Teacher, I will follow you wherever you go."* [20]*And Jesus said to him, "Foxes have holes, and birds of the air have nests; but the Son of Man has nowhere to lay his head."* [21]*Another of his disciples said to him, "Lord, first let me go and bury my father."* [22]*But Jesus said to him, "Follow me, and let the dead bury their own dead."*

[23]*And when he got into the boat, his disciples followed him.* [24]*A windstorm arose on the sea, so great that the boat was being swamped by the waves; but he was asleep.* [25]*And they went and woke him up, saying, "Lord, save us! We are perishing!"* [26]*And he said to them, "Why are you afraid, you of little faith?" Then he got up and rebuked the winds and the sea; and there was a dead calm.* [27]*They were amazed, saying, "What sort of man is this, that even the winds and the sea obey him?"*

[28]*When he came to the other side, to the country of the Gadarenes, two demoniacs coming out of the tombs met him. They were so fierce that no one could pass that way.* [29]*Suddenly they shouted, "What have you to do with us, Son of God? Have you come here to torment us before the time?"* [30]*Now a large herd of swine was feeding at some distance from them.* [31]*The demons begged him, "If*

you cast us out, send us into the herd of swine." ³²And he said to them, "Go!" So they came out and entered the swine; and suddenly, the whole herd rushed down the steep bank into the sea and perished in the water. ³³The swineherds ran off, and on going into the town, they told the whole story about what had happened to the demoniacs. ³⁴Then the whole town came out to meet Jesus; and when they saw him, they begged him to leave their neighborhood.

9 *¹And after getting into a boat he crossed the sea and came to his own town. ²And just then some people were carrying a paralyzed man lying on a bed. When Jesus saw their faith, he said to the paralytic, "Take heart, son; your sins are forgiven." ³Then some of the scribes said to themselves, "This man is blaspheming." ⁴But Jesus, perceiving their thoughts, said, "Why do you think evil in your hearts? ⁵For which is easier, to say, 'Your sins are forgiven,' or to say, 'Stand up and walk'? ⁶But so that you may know that the Son of Man has authority on earth to forgive sins" —he then said to the paralytic—"stand up, take your bed and go to your home." ⁷And he stood up and went to his home. ⁸When the crowds saw it, they were filled with awe, and they glorified God, who had given such authority to human beings.*

The healing miracles show the authority of Jesus over sickness and disease, but these miraculous deeds demonstrate his supremacy over even greater adversaries: the power of the sea, the power of demonic evil, and the power of sin. In each of these three events Jesus does things that no ordinary person can do; he does things that only God can do. Through these episodes, Matthew helps us answer the question asked by the disciples of Jesus: "What sort of man is this?"

As Jesus orders his disciples to cross to the other side of the Sea of Galilee, two different would-be disciples express a desire to go with him. The problem with both these men is that they have not sufficiently considered the cost of discipleship. Perhaps their enthusiasm is due to witnessing Jesus' miracles, but neither realizes the itinerant nature of the mission or the urgency of the call. As Jesus sets out in the boat the storm becomes a metaphor for the rigors of discipleship and a test of true discipleship.

In the Hebrew Scriptures, the stormy sea represents the forces of chaos and evil. Yet God can control this formidable power that threatens his people:

"You rule the raging of the sea; when its waves rise, you still them" (Ps 89:9). Psalm 107 depicts men who lose courage in the storm: "They cried to the Lord in their trouble, and he brought them out from their distress; he made the storm be still, and the waves of the sea were hushed" (Ps 107:28–29). The stilling of the storm provides a comforting image for disciples of all ages who are threatened by forces threatening to overwhelm them. By approaching Jesus in prayer—"Lord save us"—disciples can place their trust in his power.

As Jesus and his disciples arrive on the other side of the sea, they enter into Gentile territory, "the country of the Gadarenes" (verse 28). There Jesus is confronted by two fierce demoniacs living near the tombs and menacing any who come near. Jesus' power over the demons demonstrates the reign of God already encroaching on the domain of evil. The demons themselves request that Jesus send them into the nearby heard of swine if he casts them out of the men. Jesus utters one authoritative word, "Go!" and the demons enter the pigs, precipitating a stampede down the steep hillside and into the lake, where the entire herd drowns. When the people of the nearby town come out to Jesus, they do not praise his actions but beg him to go away. The disciples learn that the power to vanquish evil is not always welcome. Jesus complies with the town's request and returns by boat to Capernaum.

Back in "his own town," Jesus is met by people carrying a paralyzed man. Seeing their faith, Jesus says to the paralytic, "Your sins are forgiven" (9:1–2). Sin is the greatest power opposed to God's kingdom; it is the condition that holds all people bound, a state from which only God can liberate. When Jesus declares the paralytic's sins forgiven, he is accused of blasphemy, of claiming for himself an authority that belongs only to God. Jesus them heals the man as a visible demonstration of his power, leading the crowd to respond in awe and glorify God. As great as Jesus' power is to heal the sick, it pales in comparison to his authority over sin. Though sick people may be healed, they will inevitably get sick again, and ultimately they will die. Sin is at the root of all human struggles with evil, and Jesus' power to overcome the effects of sin is the heart of his mission.

One by one—through disease, the stormy sea, demons, and sin—Jesus has defeated the powers that oppress God's people by doing what only God can do. As the disciples have entered into the boat with Jesus and traveled with him back and forth across the sea, they have experienced the trials of discipleship. Matthew intends us to see ourselves in that boat with Jesus, traveling from shore to shore and encountering the oppressive powers of evil. In our struggle, we can hear the challenging but comforting question of Jesus: "Why are you afraid, you of little faith?"

Reflection and Discussion

• Can I say to Jesus, "I will follow you wherever you go"? What do I need to leave behind in order to follow Jesus more closely?

• What storms shake my life? When have I heard the voice of Jesus in the midst of the storm?

• What indicates that Jesus acts with the authority of God? In what area of my life am I most in need of the authoritative power of Jesus?

Prayer

Lord Jesus, save me. Calm the stormy waters, vanquish the evil demons, and forgive my sins. Free me from all the powers that threaten to over-whelm me. Help me to trust in you.

"I have come to call not the righteous but sinners." Matt 9:13

New Discipleship for a New Age

MATTHEW 9:9–17 *⁹As Jesus was walking along, he saw a man called Matthew sitting at the tax booth; and he said to him, "Follow me." And he got up and followed him. ¹⁰And as he sat at dinner in the house, many tax collectors and sinners came and were sitting with him and his disciples. ¹¹When the Pharisees saw this, they said to his disciples, "Why does your teacher eat with tax collectors and sinners?" ¹²But when he heard this, he said, "Those who are well have no need of a physician, but those who are sick. ¹³Go and learn what this means, 'I desire mercy, not sacrifice.' For I have come to call not the righteous but sinners."*

¹⁴Then the disciples of John came to him, saying, "Why do we and the Pharisees fast often, but your disciples do not fast?" ¹⁵And Jesus said to them, "The wedding guests cannot mourn as long as the bridegroom is with them, can they? The days will come when the bridegroom is taken away from them, and then they will fast. ¹⁶No one sews a piece of unshrunk cloth on an old cloak, for the patch pulls away from the cloak, and a worse tear is made. ¹⁷Neither is new wine put into old wineskins; otherwise, the skins burst, and the wine is spilled, and the skins are destroyed; but new wine is put into fresh wineskins, and so both are preserved."

J esus encounters Matthew working at a tax collecting station in Capernaum. This collection booth was situated near the sea so that taxes could be collected on fish or goods brought into the region by boat. In the Roman system the job of tax collector was awarded to the highest bidder. While the collector was responsible for paying a set amount to the government, he would try to collect extra taxes from the people to increase his personal profit. For this reason, the tax collectors were despised as corrupt and dishonest collaborators with the Roman government. Matthew's invitation from Jesus, like the call of the first disciples in their fishing boats, is compelling and direct, and Matthew's response is without hesitation.

The primary interest in Matthew's call comes in the subsequent verses that describe the lifestyle of Jesus and his disciples. Since sharing a meal in the Jewish culture implied a close relationship, Jesus' dining with "many tax collectors and sinners" elicits a protest from his opponents (verses 10–11). His response, in the form of a metaphor, suggests that the sinners are "sick" and need a "physician" (verse 12). It is the illness of those in sin that needs the saving medicine of God's physician. Jesus further suggests that the Pharisees reflect on the words of Hosea, "I desire mercy, not sacrifice" (Hos 6:6). This prophetic text prioritizes personal integrity and social justice over the performance of sacrificial ritual. Jesus' insistence that his opponents "go and learn" the meaning of the text suggests that they do not understand this fundamental teaching of the biblical prophets. Like the prophets before him, Jesus does not advocate abolishing the temple and the religious system that surrounds it, but understanding the greater priority of compassion and forgiveness in religious practice. Associating with sinners and outcasts and calling them to repentance become hallmarks of Jesus' ministry because those who already consider themselves righteous find it difficult to be open to his call.

The question asked of Jesus about fasting seems to concern the frequency and motivation for fasting, not the practice itself. Jesus' response that he and his disciples do not "fast often" refers to the biblical image of the wedding feast (verses 14–15). The prophets applied marriage imagery to the relationship of God and Israel, and they used the image of the banquet to express the fulfillment of Israel's hopes. Here Jesus is portrayed as the "bridegroom" of the joyful messianic banquet. Later, when Jesus is taken away, his church will return to a regular practice of fasting.

The two metaphors about patching garments and about wine and wine-skins express the reality that the coming of the Messiah has brought the law and the prophets of Israel to new and decisive fulfillment. Both images, however, express a concern for preserving the old while living in this new fullness. One would never patch an old cloak with new cloth, since the new cloth would shrink when washed and the old cloak would be torn worse than before. Likewise, one would never put new wine into old wineskins because the pressure of new fermenting wine would burst the old, brittle skins. The final result, that "both are preserved," refers not to the new wine and new container, but to the new wine and the old wineskin. Jesus does not want the cloak to tear or the old wineskin to be destroyed. Showing that both the old and the new are preserved, that Jesus is in continuity with ancient Israel, is a particular concern of Matthew and the Jewish Christians he is addressing.

Reflection and Discussion

• What does Jesus' concern for the outcasts and sinners tell me about his mission and the mission of his church today?

• Do I reach out to the sick or the healthy, the sinners or the saved? How can my life and the ministry of my faith community better reflect the priorities of Jesus?

• Why did Jesus advise the Pharisees to study the words of the prophet, "I desire mercy, not sacrifice"? How is God speaking to me through these words?

• Why does Jesus refer to himself as the "bridegroom"? How does this image help me understand his significance in my own life?

• Why is Jesus so concerned about preserving the old and the new? What are the implications of this principle for my own discipleship?

Prayer

Bridegroom of God's kingdom, you call people to the feast from all strata of society: the sinner and saint, the sick and the healthy, the outcasts and the religious elite. Broaden my vision of the kingdom and help me to follow you without reserve.

The crowds were amazed and said, "Never has anything like this been seen in Israel." Matt 9:33

A Ministry of Compassion

MATTHEW 9:18–34 ¹⁸*While he was saying these things to them, suddenly a leader of the synagogue came in and knelt before him, saying, "My daughter has just died; but come and lay your hand on her, and she will live." ¹⁹And Jesus got up and followed him, with his disciples. ²⁰Then suddenly a woman who had been suffering from hemorrhages for twelve years came up behind him and touched the fringe of his cloak, ²¹for she said to herself, "If I only touch his cloak, I will be made well." ²²Jesus turned, and seeing her he said, "Take heart, daughter; your faith has made you well." And instantly the woman was made well. ²³When Jesus came to the leader's house and saw the flute players and the crowd making a commotion, ²⁴he said, "Go away; for the girl is not dead but sleeping." And they laughed at him. ²⁵But when the crowd had been put outside, he went in and took her by the hand, and the girl got up. ²⁶And the report of this spread throughout that district.*

²⁷*As Jesus went on from there, two blind men followed him, crying loudly, "Have mercy on us, Son of David!" ²⁸When he entered the house, the blind men came to him; and Jesus said to them, "Do you believe that I am able to do this?" They said to him, "Yes, Lord." ²⁹Then he touched their eyes and said, "According to your faith let it be done to you." ³⁰And their eyes were opened. Then Jesus sternly ordered them, "See that no one knows of this." ³¹But they went away and spread the news about him throughout that district.*

71

³²*After they had gone away, a demoniac who was mute was brought to him.* ³³*And when the demon had been cast out, the one who had been mute spoke; and the crowds were amazed and said, "Never has anything like this been seen in Israel."* ³⁴*But the Pharisees said, "By the ruler of the demons he casts out the demons."*

The next series of healing stories begins with an account that sandwiches the cure of a woman who had suffered hemorrhages for many years within the account of a synagogue leader and his daughter. As the leader kneels before Jesus, he states that his daughter has died, but he also professes his belief that Jesus can lay his hand on her and raise her to life. As Jesus follows the leader to his house, the woman with the chronic hemorrhage comes up from behind and touches "the fringe of his cloak" (verse 20). The fringe refers to the blue tassels worn by Jews on the corners of their garments as a reminder to keep all of God's commandments (Num 15:38–39). The woman knows that touching the fringe will be sufficient to make her well. As Jesus approaches the house of the synagogue leader, he hears the mournful sounds of the flute and the bereavement of the crowd. The skepticism of the crowd contrasts with the faith of the girl's father. Jesus' insistence that the girl is sleeping is not a denial of her death, but rather of its finality. When Jesus takes her by the hand, the girl gets up. In both of these accounts, there is a stress on faith leading to touch as the means of healing.

As in the two previous healing accounts, the story of the two blind men places emphasis on their initiative and faith. Their cry to the Son of David emphasizes his compassion and humility amidst his messianic power. Their loud call to Jesus and their following him right into a house demonstrate their tenacious faith. The narrative also emphasizes, as do the other accounts, the touch of Jesus as an instrument of healing. The question of Jesus is directed not only to those seeking healing in the story, but also to the church addressed by Matthew, and to all of us as readers: "Do you believe that I am able to do this?" (verse 28). Every disciple must be able to respond with a confident "yes" before being sent out to share in Jesus' healing mission.

The final healing in this section of the gospel is an exorcism that leads to a cure. The root cause of the man's muteness is his demon possession, and when Jesus casts out the demon, the man speaks. The interest in this account seems to be the two opposite reactions to it. On the one hand, the crowds are amazed at the healing and consider it unprecedented in Israel. On the other hand, the religious leaders attribute his exorcism to the rule of demons. This divided response of wonder and hostility to Jesus continues to build throughout the gospel.

Reflection and Discussion

• Compare the ruler of the synagogue and the woman with the hemorrhage. In what ways are they similar?

• What are the roles of touch and faith in these healing accounts? How do both touch and faith contribute to the work of Jesus?

• How confident and persistent is my faith in Jesus? What amazes me about him?

Prayer

Son of David, you display your messianic power in humility and compassion toward those in need. Come and heal my lack of vision and my silent tongue. Help me to trust in your power to animate my life and restore my spirit.

"See, I am sending you out like sheep into the midst of wolves;
so be wise as serpents and innocent as doves." Matt 10:16

Sharing the Mission of Jesus

MATTHEW 9:35–10:23 *35 Then Jesus went about all the cities and villages, teaching in their synagogues, and proclaiming the good news of the kingdom, and curing every disease and every sickness. 36 When he saw the crowds, he had compassion for them, because they were harassed and helpless, like sheep without a shepherd. 37 Then he said to his disciples, "The harvest is plentiful, but the laborers are few; 38 therefore ask the Lord of the harvest to send out laborers into his harvest."*

10 *1 Then Jesus summoned his twelve disciples and gave them authority over unclean spirits, to cast them out, and to cure every disease and every sickness. 2 These are the names of the twelve apostles: first, Simon, also known as Peter, and his brother Andrew; James son of Zebedee, and his brother John; 3 Philip and Bartholomew; Thomas and Matthew the tax collector; James son of Alphaeus, and Thaddaeus; 4 Simon the Cananaean, and Judas Iscariot, the one who betrayed him.*

5 These twelve Jesus sent out with the following instructions: "Go nowhere among the Gentiles, and enter no town of the Samaritans, 6 but go rather to the lost sheep of the house of Israel. 7 As you go, proclaim the good news, 'The king-

dom of heaven has come near.' ⁸Cure the sick, raise the dead, cleanse the lepers, cast out demons. You received without payment; give without payment. ⁹Take no gold, or silver, or copper in your belts, ¹⁰no bag for your journey, or two tunics, or sandals, or a staff; for laborers deserve their food. ¹¹Whatever town or village you enter, find out who in it is worthy, and stay there until you leave. ¹²As you enter the house, greet it. ¹³If the house is worthy, let your peace come upon it; but if it is not worthy, let your peace return to you. ¹⁴If anyone will not welcome you or listen to your words, shake off the dust from your feet as you leave that house or town. ¹⁵Truly I tell you, it will be more tolerable for the land of Sodom and Gomorrah on the day of judgment than for that town.

¹⁶"See, I am sending you out like sheep into the midst of wolves; so be wise as serpents and innocent as doves. ¹⁷Beware of them, for they will hand you over to councils and flog you in their synagogues; ¹⁸and you will be dragged before governors and kings because of me, as a testimony to them and the Gentiles. ¹⁹When they hand you over, do not worry about how you are to speak or what you are to say; for what you are to say will be given to you at that time; ²⁰for it is not you who speak, but the Spirit of your Father speaking through you. ²¹Brother will betray brother to death, and a father his child, and children will rise against parents and have them put to death; ²²and you will be hated by all because of my name. But the one who endures to the end will be saved. ²³When they persecute you in one town, flee to the next; for truly I tell you, you will not have gone through all the towns of Israel before the Son of Man comes.

The gospel's summary of Jesus' authoritative teachings (Matt 5–7) and its summary of his authoritative deeds (Matt 8–9) present Jesus as the Messiah of Israel. His words proclaim the kingdom and his deeds actualize the kingdom. These words and deeds of Jesus (9:35) prepare for Jesus' instructions that his disciples increasingly share in his mission (Matt 10).

The compassion of Jesus for the crowds is expressed in two metaphors. The first conveys their lack of leadership (verse 36). As Moses chose Joshua to continue his mission "so that the congregation of the Lord may not be like sheep without a shepherd" (Num 27:17), Jesus chooses his twelve disciples because they are "like sheep without a shepherd." The prophecy of Ezekiel had described Israel after the exile as scattered and aimless: "My sheep were scattered over all the face of the earth, with no one to search or seek for them"

(Ezek 34:6). As in the days after the exile, God's people are now helpless and abandoned by their leaders. The second metaphor expressing the compassion of Jesus for the crowds states the urgency of the situation (verse 37). The agricultural imagery of the harvest is also rooted in the message of the prophets. God's slow work of plowing and sowing the field throughout the saving history of Israel has now reached its climactic time of harvest. The time for gathering God's people into the kingdom has arrived, but there is a shortage of laborers. This need to mobilize workers for the harvest leads into the commissioning of the twelve disciples.

The sermon to the apostles, the second of the five major discourses of the gospel, begins with Jesus summoning the twelve together (10:1). These correspond to the twelve tribes of Israel who are scattered and bereft of faithful leadership. Only here in the gospel are these twelve called "apostles" (those who are sent) rather than disciples (those who follow). These apostles become the foundational leaders of the early church, forming the bridge between the earthly ministry of Jesus and the mission of the post-resurrection church. The twelve are ordered in six pairs, with Peter designated as "first" and Judas Iscariot listed last.

The apostles' mission is directed to "the lost sheep of the house of Israel," not to the Samaritans or the Gentiles (10:5–6). The priority of Israel in God's saving plan emphasizes that the ministry of Jesus is the fulfillment of Israel's history and hope. Though the mission of the church after the resurrection will be directed to all the nations, the gospel demonstrates that the mission of Jesus is rooted in the Old Testament and the promises God made to the chosen people of the covenant. The instructions to the twelve are twofold: the ministry of word demonstrated by the ministry of deed. They must proclaim the message that Jesus announced: "The kingdom of heaven has come near" (10:7); and they must do the deeds that Jesus performed: "Cure the sick, raise the dead, cleanse the lepers, cast out demons" (10:8).

Like the sermon on the mount, this sermon to the apostles is rather loosely constructed around dominant motifs, indicating that Matthew gathered sayings of Jesus remembered from throughout his ministry and clustered them together under the theme of mission. Historically it is directed to Jesus' original apostles, but it is also aimed at the church addressed by Matthew. This open-ended relevance of the sermon extends its importance to the church in every age, offering practical guidelines for mission.

Jesus tells the disciples not to make extensive preparations for their journey, bringing no additional money or clothing (10:9–10). Their needs will be met by the support of those who hear and receive their message. This reminds disciples of Jesus in every age that their ultimate resource is his presence with them and not their own provisions. Agents of Jesus live simply, depending on him and embodying his presence. Like Jesus, their reception by others will be mixed. They will be rejected and even persecuted by some; by others they will be received and welcomed.

The tribulations experienced by disciples in their mission should come as no surprise, for they are following in the way of Jesus. Their suffering would involve persecution from both religious and secular authorities (10:17–18) as well as resistance and division within families (10:21). In the face of all this, Jesus urges his disciples to trust in the guidance of God's Spirit and in the Father's providential care.

Reflection and Discussion

• In what ways does Jesus call disciples to continue his mission? What can I do for the lost sheep of God's people today?

• What does Jesus' admonition to be "wise as serpents and innocent as doves" mean to me in the context of my discipleship?

• Why did Jesus insist that his apostles direct their mission only to the Jews, "the lost sheep of the house of Israel"?

• How have I experienced persecution, resistance, rejection, or division as a result of my discipleship? How have I been strengthened in difficulties?

• What part of Jesus' sermon to the apostles seems most applicable to the church today?

Prayer

Good Shepherd, you have compassion on your flock. Thank you for giving me a share in your mission. Guide me to be a diligent shepherd to those entrusted to me and a responsive sheep to those who guide me.

What I say to you in the dark, tell in the light; and what you hear whispered, proclaim from the housetops. Matt 10:27

Facing the Costs of Discipleship

MATTHEW 10:24–39 ²⁴*"A disciple is not above the teacher, nor a slave above the master; ²⁵it is enough for the disciple to be like the teacher, and the slave like the master. If they have called the master of the house Beelzebul, how much more will they malign those of his household!*

²⁶*"So have no fear of them; for nothing is covered up that will not be uncovered, and nothing secret that will not become known. ²⁷What I say to you in the dark, tell in the light; and what you hear whispered, proclaim from the housetops. ²⁸Do not fear those who kill the body but cannot kill the soul; rather fear him who can destroy both soul and body in hell. ²⁹Are not two sparrows sold for a penny? Yet not one of them will fall to the ground apart from your Father. ³⁰And even the hairs of your head are all counted. ³¹So do not be afraid; you are of more value than many sparrows.*

³²*"Everyone therefore who acknowledges me before others, I also will acknowledge before my Father in heaven; ³³but whoever denies me before others, I also will deny before my Father in heaven.*

³⁴*"Do not think that I have come to bring peace to the earth; I have not come to bring peace, but a sword.*

³⁵*For I have come to set a man against his father,*

and a daughter against her mother,

and a daughter-in-law against her mother-in-law;

³⁶and one's foes will be members of one's own household.

³⁷Whoever loves father or mother more than me is not worthy of me; and whoever loves son or daughter more than me is not worthy of me; ³⁸and whoever does not take up the cross and follow me is not worthy of me. ³⁹Those who find their life will lose it, and those who lose their life for my sake will find it."

T he sermon to the apostles continues with a collection of sayings directed to the church and its mission. This section begins with the assumption that underlies the entire discourse: the disciple is to be like Jesus, the master and teacher (verses 24–25). As Jesus sends out his apostles to proclaim the kingdom in word and deed, he reminds them that their identity is inextricably united with his. This unity of purpose and mission is both the basis of their authority and the guarantee of their affliction. If Jesus' opponents have tried to undermine his work by linking him with evil spirits, then the apostles should expect the same kind of persecution and denunciation.

Three times Jesus urges those he sends out on mission not to be afraid (verses 26, 28, 31). He emboldens them to have complete confidence in proclaiming God's kingdom. What Jesus has taught them privately must be proclaimed openly. The gospel is not a secret or esoteric message. What has been whispered in the darkness must come into the light and be proclaimed to all (verse 27). Because disciples share the fate of their master, they should not fear their inevitable persecution and even martyrdom because God will not allow their ultimate harm. They must have a proper fear of God, but also realize how valuable they are to God. Just as God watches over every sparrow and numbers every hair on a person's head, God's unwavering commitment enables them to trust God for their eternal welfare.

The final sayings stress the loyalty of disciples and the complete attachment to Jesus that is demanded for discipleship. A disciple's public recognition or denial of Jesus in this life anticipates Jesus' recognition or denial of the disciple in the judgment to come (verses 32–33). The message of God's kingdom is confrontational. Conflicting responses to the gospel of Jesus can splinter even the closest human bonds. Disciples must be willing to subordinate their allegiance to what they love best—even their own family—for the sake of Jesus and his mission. Jesus' purpose is not to create division, but his coming has inevitably incited conflicting responses. In essence, discipleship means to "take up the cross and follow" Jesus, which is the way to true and lasting life (verses 38–39).

Reflection and Discussion

• How do I acknowledge Jesus by my words and actions? When have I denied Jesus out of fear?

• How do I deal with my fears? What can I learn from Jesus about living more fearlessly?

• Which of these sayings of Jesus on Christian discipleship do I want to remember and carry with me?

Prayer

Lord Jesus, you encourage me to follow in your footsteps. Give me your Spirit to guide my words and strengthen my deeds. Keep me faithful to you when the going gets tough.

SUGGESTIONS FOR FACILITATORS, GROUP SESSION 4

1. Welcome group members and ask if anyone has any questions, announcements, or requests.

2. You may want to pray this prayer as a group:

Saving God, you sent Jesus to proclaim your kingdom in word and deed. His teaching and his wondrous miracles declare your desire to fulfill your promises and to conquer all powers that enslave your creation. Broaden my understanding of your kingdom and help me to be an instrument of your reign over all evil, sin, sickness, suffering, and hopeless existence. Give me the commitment to study the teachings of Jesus and the courage to follow him unreservedly. May your will be done and your kingdom come.

3. Ask one or more of the following questions:
   - What is the most difficult part of this study for you?
   - What insights stand out to you from the lessons this week?

4. Discuss lessons 13 through 18. Choose one or more of the questions for reflection and discussion from each lesson to discuss as a group. You may want to ask group members which question was most challenging or helpful to them as you review each lesson.

5. Keep the discussion moving, but allow time for the questions that provoke the most discussion. Encourage the group members to use "I" language in their responses.

6. After talking over each lesson, instruct group members to complete lessons 19 through 24 on their own during the six days before the next group meeting. They should write out their own answers to the questions as preparation for next week's session.

7. Ask the group what encouragement they need for the coming week. Ask the members to pray for the needs of one another during the week.

8. Conclude by praying aloud together the prayer at the end of one of the lessons discussed. You may choose to conclude the prayer by asking members to pray aloud any requests they may have.

**The blind receive their sight, the lame walk,
the lepers are cleansed, the deaf hear, the dead are raised,
and the poor have good news brought to them.** Matt 11:5

The Messenger Who Prepared the Way

MATTHEW 11:1–15 ¹*Now when Jesus had finished instructing his twelve disciples, he went on from there to teach and proclaim his message in their cities.*

²*When John heard in prison what the Messiah was doing, he sent word by his disciples* ³*and said to him, "Are you the one who is to come, or are we to wait for another?"* ⁴*Jesus answered them, "Go and tell John what you hear and see:* ⁵*the blind receive their sight, the lame walk, the lepers are cleansed, the deaf hear, the dead are raised, and the poor have good news brought to them.* ⁶*And blessed is anyone who takes no offense at me."*

⁷*As they went away, Jesus began to speak to the crowds about John: "What did you go out into the wilderness to look at? A reed shaken by the wind?* ⁸*What then did you go out to see? Someone dressed in soft robes? Look, those who wear soft robes are in royal palaces.* ⁹*What then did you go out to see? A prophet? Yes, I tell you, and more than a prophet.* ¹⁰*This is the one about whom it is written,*

'See, I am sending my messenger ahead of you,
who will prepare your way before you.'

¹¹Truly I tell you, among those born of women no one has arisen greater than John the Baptist; yet the least in the kingdom of heaven is greater than he. ¹²From the days of John the Baptist until now the kingdom of heaven has suffered violence, and the violent take it by force. ¹³For all the prophets and the law prophesied until John came; ¹⁴and if you are willing to accept it, he is Elijah who is to come. ¹⁵Let anyone with ears listen!

A fter his sermon addressed to the twelve apostles, Jesus again takes up his itinerant ministry throughout the cities of Galilee. Here the focus is on the divided responses to Jesus. The crowds continue to receive him favorably while the religious leaders oppose him with increasing determination. Meanwhile, the disciples continue seeking to understand Jesus and the meaning of his mission.

This section of the gospel opens with the query of John the Baptist. After Jesus has taught his disciples about the difficulties of their mission, John in prison sends his own disciples to ask Jesus if he is "the one who is to come" (verse 3). The question echoes John's earlier words, "One who is more powerful than I is coming after me" (3:11). Perhaps John has become less confident that Jesus is the Messiah due to his own imprisonment, the increasing opposition to Jesus, and the delay of God's judgment upon sin and the oppressive religious and political leaders. John's question gives Jesus an opportunity to confirm his own identity and to clarify the role of John as forerunner of the Messiah.

The response of Jesus tells John's disciples to report what they "hear," the proclamation of the kingdom and the teachings of Jesus, and what they "see," the wondrous deeds of Jesus (verse 4). The list of messianic works indicates that Jesus is fulfilling prophecies like that of Isaiah: "Then the eyes of the blind shall be opened, and the ears of the deaf unstopped; then the lame shall leap like a deer, and the tongue of the speechless sing for joy" (Isa 35:5–6). If John or anyone else is attentive to these words and deeds of Jesus, they will be "blessed" and not take offense at Jesus (verse 6). The beatitude encourages believers not to focus on the increasing opposition which leads to doubt, but to realize the presence of salvation made known in Jesus the Messiah.

Next Jesus turns to the crowds and makes a series of public statements about the significance of John's work in God's saving plan (verse 7). The images of "a reed shaken by the wind" and of "soft robes" worn in royal palaces allude to the reign of Herod Antipas, the ruler who has imprisoned John and who will have him executed. The images contrast with that of the rugged and sturdy prophet who unwaveringly challenges corrupt authority. But Jesus claims that John is even "more than a prophet" because he fulfills the role of the precursor spoken of in Malachi 3:1, the one who prepares the way for the Messiah's coming (verses 9–10).

John the Baptist lives at the conclusion of the era of God's prophets, and he will be killed by Herod shortly before Jesus' redemptive death inaugurates the new covenant. Because of John's towering role as the apex of the old covenant and the herald of the new, Jesus solemnly praises him: "Truly I tell you, among those born of women no one has arisen greater than John the Baptist" (verse 11). Yet, because John belongs only to the period of preparation for God's reign, Jesus also declares, "The least in the kingdom of heaven is greater than he." As the climactic end of the Torah and prophets, John functions in the role of Elijah, whose return was expected to herald the messianic age.

Reflection and Discussion

• Why did John the Baptist lose confidence in Jesus' identity as the one to come? What causes me to doubt the authority of Jesus?

• What convinces me that Jesus is "the one"? What are the implications of this for my life?

• In what sense does John the Baptist fulfill the role of Elijah spoken of in the last prophetic book of the Old Testament (Mal 3:1; 4:5–6)?

• How can Jesus make such seemingly contradictory statements about John the Baptist, calling him both the greatest and the least (verse 11)?

• In what sense is my life greater and more blessed than that of John the Baptist (verse 11)?

Prayer

Jesus, I believe that you are the one to come and there is no need to wait for another. Through your words and deeds, I have come to know that you are the Messiah. Help me in my struggles with doubt and let me place my trust in you.

**Take my yoke upon you, and learn from me; for I am gentle and
humble in heart, and you will find rest for your souls.
For my yoke is easy, and my burden is light.** Matt 11:29–30

Jesus Responds to Rejection

MATTHEW 11:16–30 ¹⁶*"But to what will I compare this generation? It is
like children sitting in the marketplaces and calling to one another,*

¹⁷*'We played the flute for you, and you did not dance;*
we wailed, and you did not mourn.'

¹⁸*For John came neither eating nor drinking, and they say, 'He has a demon';*
¹⁹*the Son of Man came eating and drinking, and they say, 'Look, a glutton and
a drunkard, a friend of tax collectors and sinners!' Yet wisdom is vindicated by
her deeds."*

²⁰*Then he began to reproach the cities in which most of his deeds of power had
been done, because they did not repent.* ²¹*"Woe to you, Chorazin! Woe to you,
Bethsaida! For if the deeds of power done in you had been done in Tyre and
Sidon, they would have repented long ago in sackcloth and ashes.* ²²*But I tell you,
on the day of judgment it will be more tolerable for Tyre and Sidon than for you.*
²³*And you, Capernaum,*

will you be exalted to heaven?
No, you will be brought down to Hades.

For if the deeds of power done in you had been done in Sodom, it would have remained until this day. ²⁴But I tell you that on the day of judgment it will be more tolerable for the land of Sodom than for you."

²⁵At that time Jesus said, "I thank you, Father, Lord of heaven and earth, because you have hidden these things from the wise and the intelligent and have revealed them to infants; ²⁶yes, Father, for such was your gracious will. ²⁷All things have been handed over to me by my Father; and no one knows the Son except the Father, and no one knows the Father except the Son and anyone to whom the Son chooses to reveal him.

²⁸"Come to me, all you that are weary and are carrying heavy burdens, and I will give you rest. ²⁹Take my yoke upon you, and learn from me; for I am gentle and humble in heart, and you will find rest for your souls. ³⁰For my yoke is easy, and my burden is light."

Both John the Baptist and Jesus preached the necessity of repentance in preparation for the coming of the kingdom of heaven and both were rejected by most of their contemporaries. John came as an ascetical prophet, fasting from food and water, and he was judged to be possessed by a demon (verse 18). Jesus came as the bridegroom of the wedding feast, and he was called "a glutton and a drunkard" because he dined with tax collectors and sinners (verse 19). In a provocative metaphor, Jesus compares their reception to a group of stubborn children who refuse to play either a funeral game or a wedding game (verse 17). The preaching of John is the wailing of the funeral for which they refused to mourn; the messianic work of Jesus is the flute playing at the wedding feast for which they refused to dance.

Because the preaching and powerful works of Jesus should lead to repentance, Jesus admonishes the three cities in which he had ministered (verses 20–24). Chorazin, Bethsaida, and Capernaum, all towns at the northern end of the Sea of Galilee, will receive severe judgments from God. Jesus contrasts these unrepentant Jewish villages in Galilee with three Gentile cities known for their wickedness. He suggests that Tyre, Sidon, and even notorious Sodom would have repented had they seen the powerful messianic works of Jesus. These cities outside of Israel were corrupted by their idolatry, whereas the villages of Galilee received the sustained ministry of God's Messiah.

Though Jesus experienced much rejection, many also accepted his preaching and received him. For this Jesus gives thanks to his Father, addressing him as "Lord of heaven and earth" and blending the same intimacy and reverence expressed in the Lord's Prayer (verse 25). Jesus expresses gratitude that God reveals the ways of the kingdom to "infants," those who are humble and realize their dependence on God, rather than to those who are proud and consider themselves clever and smart. This unique bond between Jesus and his Father is the source of his power and authority (verse 27). Because Jesus knows the Father so intimately, his teaching can uniquely reveal the plan and will of God to anyone to whom he chooses to reveal it.

Since the way to know the Father is through the Son, Jesus offers one of the most appealing and memorable invitations of the gospel. He calls to all who are weary and carrying heavy burdens and encourages them to come and experience the rest he offers them (verses 28–30). The invitation of Jesus is twofold. First, he says, "Come to me." Being with Jesus and sharing his life is the way to fulfillment. Next, he says, "Take my yoke upon you and learn from me." When an animal is yoked, it is ready for work. Following the teachings of Jesus and taking up the cross are certainly not effortless. Yet, Jesus says paradoxically, "My yoke is easy and my burden is light." Though the Christian life is a challenge, the way of Jesus gets at the heart of God's will for us. Because Jesus is gentle and humble, learning from him and following him is not burdensome. His way leads to rest, to his Father, to the fullness of life.

Reflection and Discussion

• Jesus' warning to the three towns of Galilee suggests that the more one has been given by God, the more one is accountable before God. In what ways does this apply to my own life?

• Do I experience my Christian life as more of a wedding dance or a funeral dirge (verse 17)? Does my faith cause me to abstain from life or enjoy its richness? Which did the lifestyle of Jesus seem to encourage?

• Why is the kingdom hidden "from the wise and intelligent" and revealed "to infants"?

• What is Jesus saying to me when he says, "My yoke is easy, and my burden is light"?

Prayer

Lord Jesus, you invite me to come to you and to learn from you the ways of the Father. As I come to you, weary and bearing heavy burdens, show me the ease and lightness of your way. I want to follow you and learn the ways of the kingdom as a humble and needy child.

He will not break a bruised reed or quench a smoldering wick until he brings justice to victory. Matt 12:20

God's Servant Is Lord of the Sabbath

MATTHEW 12:1–21 ¹*At that time Jesus went through the grainfields on the sabbath; his disciples were hungry, and they began to pluck heads of grain and to eat.* ²*When the Pharisees saw it, they said to him, "Look, your disciples are doing what is not lawful to do on the sabbath."* ³*He said to them, "Have you not read what David did when he and his companions were hungry?* ⁴*He entered the house of God and ate the bread of the Presence, which it was not lawful for him or his companions to eat, but only for the priests.* ⁵*Or have you not read in the law that on the sabbath the priests in the temple break the sabbath and yet are guiltless?* ⁶*I tell you, something greater than the temple is here.* ⁷*But if you had known what this means, 'I desire mercy and not sacrifice,' you would not have condemned the guiltless.* ⁸*For the Son of Man is lord of the sabbath."*

⁹*He left that place and entered their synagogue;* ¹⁰*a man was there with a withered hand, and they asked him, "Is it lawful to cure on the sabbath?" so that they might accuse him.* ¹¹*He said to them, "Suppose one of you has only one sheep and it falls into a pit on the sabbath; will you not lay hold of it and lift it out?* ¹²*How much more valuable is a human being than a sheep! So it is lawful to do good on the sabbath."* ¹³*Then he said to the man, "Stretch out your hand." He stretched it out, and it was restored, as sound as the other.* ¹⁴*But the Pharisees*

went out and conspired against him, how to destroy him.

[15] When Jesus became aware of this, he departed. Many crowds followed him, and he cured all of them, [16] and he ordered them not to make him known. [17] This was to fulfill what had been spoken through the prophet Isaiah:

[18] "Here is my servant, whom I have chosen,
     my beloved, with whom my soul is well pleased.
I will put my Spirit upon him,
     and he will proclaim justice to the Gentiles.
[19] He will not wrangle or cry aloud,
     nor will anyone hear his voice in the streets.
[20] He will not break a bruised reed
     or quench a smoldering wick
until he brings justice to victory.
     [21] And in his name the Gentiles will hope."

These two controversies between Jesus and his opponents seem to be, on the surface, a dispute about interpretation of the Torah precept instructing Israel to honor the Sabbath. Discussions about what was allowable during the Sabbath rest were frequent among Jewish leaders at the time. The rabbis would later codify specific prohibitions to safeguard the sanctity of the Sabbath as a day of complete rest. It was a common understanding among Jewish teachers, however, that all restrictive laws were superseded in the presence of human emergency: disaster, self-defense, peril to life and limb, and the like. The rigorous Sabbath rest was moderated by a principle stated by a rabbi of the second century but which most Jews at the time of Jesus already understood: "The Sabbath was delivered to you, and not you to the Sabbath."

Jesus cited two biblical examples in defense of his disciples who were hungry and picked grain on the Sabbath. The first is that of David and his men who entered the temple and ate the sacred bread that had been set aside for the rituals of the priests (verses 3–4). David's procuring the bread was an act of compassion for his hungry followers that superseded the regulations of the temple. Jesus did for his disciples what David did for his companions. The second example is that of the priests of the temple who are required to perform certain duties on the Sabbath (verse 5). Their obligations override the general law prescribing rest on the Sabbath. Again, Jesus expresses God's will as expressed by the prophet Hosea, "I desire mercy and not sacrifice" (verse 6). In giving priority to human need, Jesus does not disregard the law, but interprets it in a way that fulfills its God-given intent.

The next controversy occurs on the same Sabbath as Jesus enters the synagogue and encounters a man with a withered hand (verses 9–10). Wishing to entrap Jesus and find evidence with which to accuse him in court, his opponents ask whether it is lawful to cure on the Sabbath. By offering the example of the sheep falling into the pit on the Sabbath, Jesus argues for the general principle that "it is lawful to do good on the Sabbath" (verse 12). If an animal could be rescued on the Sabbath, how much more lawful should it be to liberate a human being? Again, Jesus interprets the precept in a way that does not violate the Torah but authoritatively relates Sabbath law and human need.

These two conflicts are about much more, however, than strict or lenient interpretations of the law. Jesus' interpretations are due to his supreme authority as one who is greater than David, the temple, and the Sabbath. Jesus solemnly declares, "I tell you, something greater than the temple is here," and "the Son of Man is lord of the Sabbath." As God's Messiah, the bearer of the kingdom, he has brought all the sacred institutions of Israel to their fullest expression. Jesus' defense of his disciples when they are accused of traveling and picking grain on the Sabbath is due to the urgency of their mission in proclaiming the kingdom of God. Jesus' healing on the Sabbath expresses the kingdom he has come to bring.

Jesus' teaching about the Sabbath expresses the Jewish belief that the Sabbath anticipates the messianic age. It is a foretaste of God's kingdom, and anticipation in the present world of the world to come. The coming day of perfect peace, healing, and joy is foreshadowed in God's gift of the Sabbath. For that reason, the rabbis taught that people should conduct themselves on the Sabbath as if the future time were already at hand. Jesus traveled and healed on the Sabbath, not to violate the law or to show that he was above the law, but to link his ministry with that day which symbolized the future kingdom he had come to bring. With Jesus, the kingdom is at hand, as he brings the blessedness and wholeness that had long been associated with the Sabbath.

The final excerpt is Matthew's longest fulfillment passage (verses 18–21). Jesus is God's servant as proclaimed by the prophet Isaiah, the servant upon whom God has given his Spirit. His Spirit-empowered ministry is characterized by deeds of justice rather than inflammatory words. He will handle the weak ones, the injured reeds and the flickering wicks, with compassionate care. In this way he will bring about justice, not only to Israel but to the Gentiles throughout the earth.

Reflection and Discussion

• Why did Jesus choose to heal people on the Sabbath when he could have chosen any other day?

• Do I understand that rest from work is an important religious obligation? What principle do I use to determine what to do and what not to do on the Lord's Day?

• How do I experience the Lord's Day as an anticipation in the present world of the coming kingdom of God?

Prayer

Lord of the Sabbath, you rested each week and set aside time dedicated to the Father. Help me to break from the endless pursuit of accomplishments and surrender my time to you.

If it is by the Spirit of God that I cast out demons, then the kingdom of God has come to you. Matt 12:28

A Messiah Greater than Jonah and Solomon

MATTHEW 12:22–42 *²²Then they brought to him a demoniac who was blind and mute; and he cured him, so that the one who had been mute could speak and see. ²³All the crowds were amazed and said, "Can this be the Son of David?" ²⁴But when the Pharisees heard it, they said, "It is only by Beelzebul, the ruler of the demons, that this fellow casts out the demons." ²⁵He knew what they were thinking and said to them, "Every kingdom divided against itself is laid waste, and no city or house divided against itself will stand. ²⁶If Satan casts out Satan, he is divided against himself; how then will his kingdom stand? ²⁷If I cast out demons by Beelzebul, by whom do your own exorcists cast them out? Therefore they will be your judges. ²⁸But if it is by the Spirit of God that I cast out demons, then the kingdom of God has come to you. ²⁹Or how can one enter a strong man's house and plunder his property, without first tying up the strong man? Then indeed the house can be plundered. ³⁰Whoever is not with me is against me, and whoever does not gather with me scatters. ³¹Therefore I tell you, people will be forgiven for every sin and blasphemy, but blasphemy against the Spirit will not be forgiven. ³²Whoever speaks a word against the Son of Man will be forgiven, but whoever speaks against the Holy Spirit will not be forgiven, either in this age or in the age to come.*

³³"Either make the tree good, and its fruit good; or make the tree bad, and its fruit bad; for the tree is known by its fruit. ³⁴You brood of vipers! How can you speak good things, when you are evil? For out of the abundance of the heart the mouth speaks. ³⁵The good person brings good things out of a good treasure, and the evil person brings evil things out of an evil treasure. ³⁶I tell you, on the day of judgment you will have to give an account for every careless word you utter; ³⁷for by your words you will be justified, and by your words you will be con-demned."

³⁸Then some of the scribes and Pharisees said to him, "Teacher, we wish to see a sign from you." ³⁹But he answered them, "An evil and adulterous generation asks for a sign, but no sign will be given to it except the sign of the prophet Jonah. ⁴⁰For just as Jonah was three days and three nights in the belly of the sea mon-ster, so for three days and three nights the Son of Man will be in the heart of the earth. ⁴¹The people of Nineveh will rise up at the judgment with this generation and condemn it, because they repented at the proclamation of Jonah, and see, something greater than Jonah is here! ⁴²The queen of the South will rise up at the judgment with this generation and condemn it, because she came from the ends of the earth to listen to the wisdom of Solomon, and see, something greater than Solomon is here!"

When Jesus heals the blind and mute demoniac, conflict arises over the origin of his power. There is no doubt about the wondrous works of Jesus; the debate is over their source. The crowds won-der whether Jesus is the Son of David, the Messiah, while the opponents of Jesus say that his power comes from Satan (verses 23–24). The response of Jesus is an extended teaching on the Holy Spirit as the source of his work. The wondrous deeds of Jesus are a blow against the kingdom of Satan and a sign that the kingdom of God has arrived (verse 28). Jesus compares the encroach-ment of God's kingdom into Satan's domain to binding a strong man in order to enter his house and plunder his property (verse 29). In the battle between the messianic kingdom and the demonic kingdom, neutrality and observation from the sidelines are impossible (verse 30). Though Satan's power is being shattered by the power of Christ, he is still an effective enemy and will be totally incapacitated only in the future.

Jesus affirms that God's mercy is all-encompassing, and every sin that people commit can be forgiven except for one—"blasphemy against the Spirit" (verse 31). Even those who insult and reject Jesus, out of ignorance, obstinacy, or fear, can be forgiven. But those who willfully reject the work of the Holy Spirit refuse to accept God's healing mercy and cannot be forgiven. Though God offers his forgiveness to everyone, no matter what their sin, refusing forgiveness means remaining unforgiven.

Since the works of Jesus could come only from God or Satan—there is no middle ground—Jesus calls on his opponents to be consistent in judging him and his deeds. Since curing the sick and expelling demons are good actions, then Jesus himself must be good. For a good tree produces good fruit and a bad tree brings forth bad fruit (verse 33). But since the Pharisees speak slanderous words against Jesus out of corrupt and evil hearts, their words are like the worthless fruit of a useless tree. Jesus reminds all his listeners that they will be judged ultimately by the words that come from the treasury of the heart: Good words that flow from a good heart will vindicate good people, but evil words from an evil heart will condemn evil people (verse 37).

When the opponents of Jesus demand to see "a sign," probably some spectacular proof of his authority, Jesus is exasperated with them and realizes that they will want an ever greater sign no matter what sign he provides. He states that their only manifestation will be "the sign of the prophet Jonah" (verses 39–40). The journey of Jonah in the belly of the sea creature and his safe release on dry land after three days foreshadow the entombment and resurrection of Jesus. Although the people of Nineveh repented when Jonah preached to them, Jesus' hearers fail to repent at the message of the kingdom. Jesus also recalls the visit of the Queen of Sheba to hear the wisdom of King Solomon (verse 42). Even though the Ninevites and the Queen were foreign Gentiles, they responded positively to Jonah and Solomon. But the Messiah is far superior to these. Jesus is a greater prophet than Jonah and a wiser king than Solomon. Indeed, he is the fullest expression of Israel's priests, prophets, and kings. The rest of the Sabbath, the priestly offerings in the temple, and the prophetic promises to David—these all have their fulfillment in Israel's Messiah.

Reflection and Discussion

• What are the signs around me that the kingdom of God is present, and that the kingdom of Satan is being overturned?

• Why is "the unforgivable sin" not a matter of God's desire to forgive but of human acceptance of God's forgiveness? Why is it impossible for this one sin to be forgiven?

• What do the people of Nineveh and the Queen of Sheba teach me about how to respond to Jesus?

Prayer

Messiah and Lord, you are greater than the prophets, higher than the temple, and wiser than Solomon. Help me to recognize the gift of God's kingdom and to manifest its presence in my world today.

**Truly I tell you, many prophets and righteous people
longed to see what you see, but did not see it,
and to hear what you hear, but did not hear it.** Matt 13:17

Revealing the Secrets
of the Kingdom

MATTHEW 13:1—23 ¹*That same day Jesus went out of the house and sat
beside the sea. ²Such great crowds gathered around him that he got into a boat
and sat there, while the whole crowd stood on the beach. ³And he told them
many things in parables, saying: "Listen! A sower went out to sow. ⁴And as he
sowed, some seeds fell on the path, and the birds came and ate them up. ⁵Other
seeds fell on rocky ground, where they did not have much soil, and they sprang
up quickly, since they had no depth of soil. ⁶But when the sun rose, they were
scorched; and since they had no root, they withered away. ⁷Other seeds fell
among thorns, and the thorns grew up and choked them. ⁸Other seeds fell on
good soil and brought forth grain, some a hundredfold, some sixty, some thirty.
⁹Let anyone with ears listen!"*

¹⁰*Then the disciples came and asked him, "Why do you speak to them in
parables?" ¹¹He answered, "To you it has been given to know the secrets of the
kingdom of heaven, but to them it has not been given. ¹²For to those who have,
more will be given, and they will have an abundance; but from those who have
nothing, even what they have will be taken away. ¹³The reason I speak to them
in parables is that 'seeing they do not perceive, and hearing they do not listen,*

nor do they understand.' ¹⁴With them indeed is fulfilled the prophecy of Isaiah
that says:

> *'You will indeed listen, but never understand,*
> > *and you will indeed look, but never perceive.*
> ¹⁵*For this people's heart has grown dull,*
> > *and their ears are hard of hearing,*
> > > *and they have shut their eyes;*
> > *so that they might not look with their eyes,*
> *and listen with their ears,*
> *and understand with their heart and turn—*
> > *and I would heal them.'*

¹⁶*But blessed are your eyes, for they see, and your ears, for they hear.* ¹⁷*Truly I*
tell you, many prophets and righteous people longed to see what you see, but did
not see it, and to hear what you hear, but did not hear it.

    ¹⁸*"Hear then the parable of the sower.* ¹⁹*When anyone hears the word of the*
kingdom and does not understand it, the evil one comes and snatches away what
is sown in the heart; this is what was sown on the path. ²⁰*As for what was sown*
on rocky ground, this is the one who hears the word and immediately receives it
with joy; ²¹*yet such a person has no root, but endures only for a while, and when*
trouble or persecution arises on account of the word, that person immediately
falls away. ²²*As for what was sown among thorns, this is the one who hears the*
word, but the cares of the world and the lure of wealth choke the word, and it
yields nothing. ²³*But as for what was sown on good soil, this is the one who hears*
the word and understands it, who indeed bears fruit and yields, in one case a
hundredfold, in another sixty, and in another thirty."

T his chapter forms the third major discourse of Matthew's gospel and
consists of seven parables. Teaching in parables was characteristic of
Jesus. He valued the ability of parables to seize the attention of his
hearers and open their minds to new ideas. Parables both surprise and disturb
listeners, posing questions with which they must struggle, and in that effort
arrive at new understandings. This mysterious and multivalent character of
the parables makes them an extension of the gradually unfolding mystery of
Jesus himself. They help to intensify the central theme of Matthew's gospel
that the kingdom of God has come in Jesus.

As Jesus begins to teach, he is seated in a boat on the sea while the listening crowd stands on the shore (verse 2). The images Jesus uses, concerning seeds and harvests, are familiar ones within the agricultural society he addresses. He teaches in parables in order to reveal the truths of the kingdom to his disciples and to conceal these truths from his opponents. Jesus quotes from Isaiah to explain the opponents' refusal to understand him: "This people's heart has grown dull" (verse 15). They have shut their eyes and their ears so they cannot understand with their hearts. Conversely, as the parable states, a disciple is "the one who hears the word and understands it" (verse 23). These are truly "blessed" because they are privileged to be alive at his time in order to witness the dawn of the messianic kingdom (verse 16–17).

As Jesus explains the parable, he himself is the one who sows "the word of the kingdom," and the ground on which the seed falls represents four different kinds of hearers of God's word. One kind hears only superficially and is easily led astray (verse 19). Another hears only in a fickle way, so that initial enthusiasm finds itself without stable roots to endure difficulties and persecution (verse 21). Another is led astray by anxieties and the lure of wealth (verse 22). The final kind hears the word of God's kingdom, acts upon it, and flourishes. The first three kinds fail to produce anything of lasting value, but the true disciple produces an abundant yield.

Jesus' parables describe the response of the people of Israel to his message of the kingdom. But after his resurrection, the parables will just as accurately describe the response of the people of the world to the message of Christ's church. The images of seeds and harvest express the interrelationship of God's grace and human choice. Whether those who hear the word try to understand it deeply and hold on to it in challenging times is largely a matter of human choice, but the word itself has a divine capacity to grow wherever it is planted. Bearing fruit is the crucial test of genuine discipleship, but notice that there are different degrees of fruit-bearing: some bear a hundredfold, some sixty, and some thirty. Mature discipleship does not happen instantly, since discipleship, like fruit-bearing, requires a growing season before there can be a harvest.

Reflection and Discussion

• How has my response to God's word been like the four types of hearers in the parable?

• What do I need to do in order to plow the soil so that God's word will flourish?

• If I focus on the one who sows the seed rather than the type of soil that receives it, what does the fact that he indiscriminately sows seeds on every type of ground tell me about Jesus?

Prayer

Creator God, you have planted the seeds of your kingdom in the fields of our world. Till the soil of my life so that your word will bring forth a rich harvest within the context of my world.

"I will open my mouth to speak in parables; I will proclaim
what has been hidden from the foundation of the world." Matt 13:35

Parables of the Kingdom

MATTHEW 13:24–53 [24]*He put before them another parable: "The kingdom of
heaven may be compared to someone who sowed good seed in his field;* [25]*but while
everybody was asleep, an enemy came and sowed weeds among the wheat, and
then went away.* [26]*So when the plants came up and bore grain, then the weeds
appeared as well.* [27]*And the slaves of the householder came and said to him, 'Master,
did you not sow good seed in your field? Where, then, did these weeds come from?'*
[28]*He answered, 'An enemy has done this.' The slaves said to him, 'Then do you want
us to go and gather them?'* [29]*But he replied, 'No; for in gathering the weeds you
would uproot the wheat along with them.* [30]*Let both of them grow together until the
harvest; and at harvest time I will tell the reapers, Collect the weeds first and bind
them in bundles to be burned, but gather the wheat into my barn.'"*

[31]*He put before them another parable: "The kingdom of heaven is like a mustard seed that someone took and sowed in his field;* [32]*it is the smallest of all the
seeds, but when it has grown it is the greatest of shrubs and becomes a tree, so
that the birds of the air come and make nests in its branches."*

[33]*He told them another parable: "The kingdom of heaven is like yeast that a
woman took and mixed in with three measures of flour until all of it was leavened."*

[34]*Jesus told the crowds all these things in parables; without a parable he told them
nothing.* [35]*This was to fulfill what had been spoken through the prophet:*

"I will open my mouth to speak in parables;

   I will proclaim what has been hidden from the foundation of the world."

³⁶*Then he left the crowds and went into the house. And his disciples approached him, saying, "Explain to us the parable of the weeds of the field."* ³⁷*He answered, "The one who sows the good seed is the Son of Man;* ³⁸*the field is the world, and the good seed are the children of the kingdom; the weeds are the children of the evil one,* ³⁹*and the enemy who sowed them is the devil; the harvest is the end of the age, and the reapers are angels.* ⁴⁰*Just as the weeds are collected and burned up with fire, so will it be at the end of the age.* ⁴¹*The Son of Man will send his angels, and they will collect out of his kingdom all causes of sin and all evildoers,* ⁴²*and they will throw them into the furnace of fire, where there will be weeping and gnashing of teeth.* ⁴³*Then the righteous will shine like the sun in the kingdom of their Father. Let anyone with ears listen!*

⁴⁴*"The kingdom of heaven is like treasure hidden in a field, which someone found and hid; then in his joy he goes and sells all that he has and buys that field.*

⁴⁵*"Again, the kingdom of heaven is like a merchant in search of fine pearls;* ⁴⁶*on finding one pearl of great value, he went and sold all that he had and bought it.*

⁴⁷*"Again, the kingdom of heaven is like a net that was thrown into the sea and caught fish of every kind;* ⁴⁸*when it was full, they drew it ashore, sat down, and put the good into baskets but threw out the bad.* ⁴⁹*So it will be at the end of the age. The angels will come out and separate the evil from the righteous* ⁵⁰*and throw them into the furnace of fire, where there will be weeping and gnashing of teeth.*

⁵¹*"Have you understood all this?" They answered, "Yes."* ⁵²*And he said to them, "Therefore every scribe who has been trained for the kingdom of heaven is like the master of a household who brings out of his treasure what is new and what is old."* ⁵³*When Jesus had finished these parables, he left that place.*

The subject matter of the remaining six parables is God's reign, which Jesus has come to bring. Each parable begins with the words, "The kingdom of heaven is like…" Jesus speaks to the crowds in parables in order to reveal to them the mystery of God's kingdom that has been "hidden from the foundation of the world" (verse 35). It is this kingdom and its mysteries that Jesus both teaches and embodies.

The first and last parables, the story of the weeds in the wheat (verses 24–30) and that of the net thrown into the sea (verses 47–50), deal with the mystery of the acceptance and rejection of Jesus' word of the kingdom. The parables assure the hearers that a separation of the children of the kingdom and the children of the evil one will occur, but they warn that now is not the time for judgment. The weeds should be allowed to grow with the wheat until harvest time; the fish should not be separated until the net is full and hauled ashore. The human tendency is to want to set things aright immediately, but Jesus urges his hearers to be patient and wait for God's judgment.

The twin parables of the mustard seed and of the yeast speak about the mysterious growth of God's kingdom. The tiny seed becomes a large bush (verses 31–32); the batch of dough becomes leavened bread (verse 33). Despite the significant expansion, still these images of the kingdom are simple: the backyard herb and common bread. The parable demonstrates how the grace of God's kingdom is working gradually but significantly, in ways that are often hidden. The subtle yet real influence of the kingdom permeates the world and offers hope.

The parables of the treasure in the field and the valuable pearl convey the fact that the value of God's kingdom makes its attainment worthy of the greatest risk. The treasure is found unexpectedly; the pearl is discovered after a diligent search. But, in both cases, the ones who find the treasure and the pearl sell all that they have to attain the precious discovery (verses 44–46). The emphasis, however, is not on how much one has to give up, but on the joy that comes from the complete investment of self and resources in God's kingdom. Discipleship means seeking first the kingdom of God and complete devotion to it.

In this third of the five discourses of Matthew's gospel, Jesus has taught his disciples about the kingdom through the means of parables. As he concludes, he asks them if they have understood, and they answer affirmatively. This means of teaching has been effective for those to whom it has been given to understand "the secrets of the kingdom of heaven" (13:11). They have been taught that the kingdom will have a mixed reception until the end of the age. The kingdom will grow, often imperceptibly, and those who commit themselves to it unreservedly will triumph in the end. As the disciples continue to grow in their responsibility for the community established by Jesus, they become scribes "trained for the kingdom of heaven" (verse 52). Like a homeowner who draws upon both new and old resources in managing the household, the disciples must keep faith with the Torah and prophets of Israel while boldly proclaiming the fulfilled and definitive teachings of Jesus. In the church to which Matthew's gospel is addressed, the leaders must represent a Christianity encompassing both the old covenant and the new.

Reflection and Discussion

• Which of these parables of Jesus opens my eyes to see in a new way? What are the insights it offers me?

• Only when the fruit appears on the wheat can it be distinguished from the weeds. In what way does this parable encourage careful discernment, patience, and tolerance?

• When have I experienced the joy described in the parable of the buried treasure and the valuable pearl?

Prayer

Lord of the harvest, unburden me of the need to set things right and help me to trust that all will be right in your time. May I seek first your kingdom and rejoice in the priceless gift you have given me.

SUGGESTIONS FOR FACILITATORS, GROUP SESSION 5

1. Welcome group members and ask if anyone has any questions, announcements, or requests.

2. You may want to pray this prayer as a group:

Almighty God, you have sent your Son to teach and live the ways of your kingdom in the world. As scribes of your kingdom, may we honor the temple sacrifices, the words of the prophets, and the rule of David's line, but recognize that your Son is greater than the temple, prophets, and kings of old. We come to learn from him as meek and hungry children, eager to receive the gift of your kingdom and manifest its presence in the world. Help us to seek your reign as the first priority of our lives and to rejoice in this priceless gift.

3. Ask one or more of the following questions:
   - What most intrigued you from this week's study?
   - What makes you want to know and understand more of God's word?

4. Discuss lessons 19 through 24. Choose one or more of the questions for reflection and discussion from each lesson to talk over as a group.

5. Ask the group members to name one thing they have most appreciated about the way the group has worked during this Bible study. Ask group members to discuss any changes they might suggest in the way the group works in future studies.

6. Invite group members to complete lessons 25 through 30 on their own during the six days before the next meeting. They should write out their own answers to the questions as preparation for next week's session.

7. Ask group members why they think that parables are such an effective form of teaching and why Jesus might have taught in parables so often.

8. Conclude by praying aloud together the prayer at the end of one of the lessons discussed. You may want to conclude the prayer by asking members to voice prayers of thanksgiving.

When Herod's birthday came, the daughter of Herodias danced
before the company, and she pleased Herod so much that
he promised on oath to grant her whatever she might ask. Matt 14:6–7

Rejection of Jesus and Execution of His Messenger

MATTHEW 14:1–12 ¹*At that time Herod the ruler heard reports about Jesus;* ²*and he said to his servants, "This is John the Baptist; he has been raised from the dead, and for this reason these powers are at work in him."* ³*For Herod had arrested John, bound him, and put him in prison on account of Herodias, his brother Philip's wife,* ⁴*because John had been telling him, "It is not lawful for you to have her."* ⁵*Though Herod wanted to put him to death, he feared the crowd, because they regarded him as a prophet.* ⁶*But when Herod's birthday came, the daughter of Herodias danced before the company, and she pleased Herod* ⁷*so much that he promised on oath to grant her whatever she might ask.* ⁸*Prompted by her mother, she said, "Give me the head of John the Baptist here on a platter."* ⁹*The king was grieved, yet out of regard for his oaths and for the guests, he commanded it to be given;* ¹⁰*he sent and had John beheaded in the prison.* ¹¹*The head was brought on a platter and given to the girl, who brought it to her mother.* ¹²*His disciples came and took the body and buried it; then they went and told Jesus.*

John the Baptist is a significant presence in Matthew's gospel, with references to his activity interspersed within the narrative of Jesus. After describing his baptismal ministry at the Jordan (3:1–17), the gospel notes his arrest as Jesus withdraws to Galilee (4:12), and reports John's question about Jesus from prison (11:2). The gospel has described John as a daring prophet, unafraid of the ruling powers. The parallels with the life of Jesus are significant: Both preach repentance and the coming of God's kingdom, both experience ridicule and rejection (11:18–19), and both are ultimately arrested and put to death by the ruling powers. The message and the destiny of John and Jesus are inseparably linked.

Herod's interest in Jesus leads to the flashback that occupies most of this account (verses 3–12). Herod has arrested John the Baptist for denouncing his marriage to Herodias. Herod had divorced his first wife in order to marry Herodias, who was formerly married to his half-brother Philip. The marriage violated Jewish law forbidding incestuous marriage to the wife of one's living brother. Although Herod wanted to have John put to death, he feared the crowd's response to the execution of a man they believed to be a prophet. Herodias also resented John and desired his death. When her daughter's dance at Herod's birthday celebration led to his impulsive promise, Herodias prompted her daughter to ask for a monstrous reward, "Give me the head of John the Baptist here on a platter." Although Herod regretted his rash oath, his desire not to lose face with his guests and his desire for harmony with his second wife overcame his fears. John was beheaded without a trial, and the morbid scene at the party was played out. John's disciples were devoted to the end, caring for his body, burying it, and informing Jesus of John's demise.

As Herod hears the news about Jesus' ministry in Galilee, he is convinced that Jesus is John the Baptist raised from the dead (verses 1–2). Herod's bizarre and guilt-ridden conclusion underlines the link between the lives and deaths of John and Jesus. Herod's reluctance to execute John anticipates Pilate's reluctance to have Jesus put to death. Although beheading was not as horrid as crucifixion, it was nevertheless a shameful way to die. As the gospel portrays John's death as a prophet at the hands of a corrupt tyrant, the reader realizes that a similar martyr's death awaits Jesus. Furthermore, Herod's mistaken speculation that Jesus is John the Baptist raised from the dead ironically points to the truth that even violent death cannot silence the voice of either John or Jesus.

Reflection and Discussion

• Why did Herod have John beheaded? What does this say about Herod's character?

• What were some of Herod's fears? When have my actions been governed by my fears?

• The similarities between John the Baptist and Jesus are uncanny. How does the fate of John the Baptist point toward that of Jesus?

Prayer

Lord Jesus, the shallow personality and shamefaced fears of Herod prompted him to execute John the Baptist. Help me to develop a confident character and a fearless discipleship so that I can face with courage the challenges of following you.

Peter answered him, "Lord, if it is you, command me to come to you on the water." He said, "Come." So Peter got out of the boat, started walking on the water, and came toward Jesus. Matt 14:28–29

The Messiah Feeds the Multitudes and Walks on the Sea

MATTHEW 14:13–33 *13Now when Jesus heard this, he withdrew from there in a boat to a deserted place by himself. But when the crowds heard it, they followed him on foot from the towns. 14When he went ashore, he saw a great crowd; and he had compassion for them and cured their sick. 15When it was evening, the disciples came to him and said, "This is a deserted place, and the hour is now late; send the crowds away so that they may go into the villages and buy food for themselves." 16Jesus said to them, "They need not go away; you give them something to eat." 17They replied, "We have nothing here but five loaves and two fish." 18And he said, "Bring them here to me." 19Then he ordered the crowds to sit down on the grass. Taking the five loaves and the two fish, he looked up to heaven, and blessed and broke the loaves, and gave them to the disciples, and the disciples gave them to the crowds. 20And all ate and were filled; and they took up what was left over of the broken pieces, twelve baskets full. 21And those who ate were about five thousand men, besides women and children.*

²²*Immediately he made the disciples get into the boat and go on ahead to the other side, while he dismissed the crowds.* ²³*And after he had dismissed the crowds, he went up the mountain by himself to pray. When evening came, he was there alone,* ²⁴*but by this time the boat, battered by the waves, was far from the land, for the wind was against them.* ²⁵*And early in the morning he came walking toward them on the sea.* ²⁶*But when the disciples saw him walking on the sea, they were terrified, saying, "It is a ghost!" And they cried out in fear.* ²⁷*But immediately Jesus spoke to them and said, "Take heart, it is I; do not be afraid."* ²⁸*Peter answered him, "Lord, if it is you, command me to come to you on the water."* ²⁹*He said, "Come." So Peter got out of the boat, started walking on the water, and came toward Jesus.* ³⁰*But when he noticed the strong wind, he became frightened, and beginning to sink, he cried out, "Lord, save me!"* ³¹*Jesus immediately reached out his hand and caught him, saying to him, "You of little faith, why did you doubt?"* ³²*When they got into the boat, the wind ceased.* ³³*And those in the boat worshiped him, saying, "Truly you are the Son of God."*

Throughout the Scriptures, meals express relationships. The anticipated kingdom of God is imagined by the prophets as a great meal of rich foods and fine wines served by God to all his people. The bountiful meal Jesus holds for the hungry crowds is quite a contrast to the birthday bash held for Herod and his court. Herod's banquet was filled with scheming, and resulted in a rash promise and murder; Jesus' feast is filled with trust, and results in generosity and satisfaction.

When the disciples suggest that Jesus dismiss the crowd so they can go eat, Jesus tells the disciples to feed the people themselves. As if to set an example for his disciples to follow, Jesus feeds the hungry crowd with five loaves and two fish. The wondrous feast looks back to what God did through Moses and the prophets. The note that the feeding took place in "a deserted place" evokes images of God feeding the Israelites in the wilderness with manna and quail through the mediation of Moses. The feeding of hungry people with meager provisions recalls the story of Elisha the prophet who told his servant to feed a hundred hungry men with twenty barley loaves and a few ears of grain. Despite the servant's skepticism, all were fed, with some left over, "according to the word of the Lord" (2 Kgs 4:42–44). The feeding of the crowd also looks forward to the Last Supper and the church's Eucharist. Jesus' sequence of actions—taking, blessing, breaking, and giving the bread (verse 19)—anticipates the same gestures of Jesus' final meal with his disciples.

After spending the night alone on the mountain in prayer, Jesus came walking across the water of the sea toward his disciples' boat as it tossed in the wind and the waves. Amidst the howling wind and the labored breath of the rowers, the disciples saw a singular physical presence shrouded in darkness moving toward them. Terrified and imagining it was a ghost, the disciples cried out in fear. Jesus immediately reassured them that he was there to rescue them from the peril of the sea.

The scene is both a revelation of Jesus' divine nature and a manifestation of his power to save. The Old Testament abounds in texts of divine rescue from storm as well as manifestations of divine power over the sea. Jesus' words, "It is I" (verse 27) are literally translated "I Am," the self-designation of God throughout the Hebrew Scriptures. The divine name, accompanied by the divine command, "Do not be afraid," frequently expresses God's desire to save his people from danger.

Peter's audacious attempt to walk upon the sea demonstrates Jesus' ability to both empower and to rescue his premier disciple. It is only divine authority that can enable a man to walk on water. Peter walked on the troubled sea as he depended on Jesus, as he trusted him and let him take charge. Yet Peter began to sink when the wind and the waves began to overwhelm him, as he took his focus off Jesus. Peter cried out, "Lord, save me!" and the hand of Jesus was immediately there to hold him up. How far had Peter walked on the water before he began to fail? How deep had he sunk before Jesus reached out his hand? Matthew's gospel is not concerned with such details. The important reality is that Peter stepped out in faith and walked on the sea and that Jesus rescued him when Peter was overcome with fear.

Reflection and Discussion

• In what ways does Jesus emphasize the role of his disciples in the feeding account? What lesson is he teaching them?

• The feeding with the five loaves and two fish looks backward to God's feeding his people with manna and quail in the wilderness and it looks forward to the Eucharist of the church. In what ways does Matthew alert readers to this backward and foward look?

• What did Peter learn about himself and about Jesus from his experience with Jesus on the tossing sea?

• Would I more likely stay in the boat or step out of it? In what way does Jesus call me to a more fearless life?

Prayer

Son of God, you went up to the mountain by yourself to pray. As I live out my discipleship, calm my fears and save me from distress. Help me to trust that you will feed me when I am hungry and rescue me when I am drowning.

"It is not what goes into the mouth that defiles a person,
but it is what comes out of the mouth that defiles." Matt 15:11

Dispute over What Pollutes a Person

MATTHEW 15:1–20 ¹*Then Pharisees and scribes came to Jesus from Jerusalem and said,* ²*"Why do your disciples break the tradition of the elders? For they do not wash their hands before they eat."* ³*He answered them, "And why do you break the commandment of God for the sake of your tradition?* ⁴*For God said, 'Honor your father and your mother,' and, 'Whoever speaks evil of father or mother must surely die.'* ⁵*But you say that whoever tells father or mother, 'Whatever support you might have had from me is given to God,' then that person need not honor the father.* ⁶*So, for the sake of your tradition, you make void the word of God.* ⁷*You hypocrites! Isaiah prophesied rightly about you when he said:*

⁸*'This people honors me with their lips,*
but their hearts are far from me;
⁹*in vain do they worship me,*
teaching human precepts as doctrines.'"

¹⁰*Then he called the crowd to him and said to them, "Listen and understand:* ¹¹*it is not what goes into the mouth that defiles a person, but it is what comes out of the mouth that defiles."* ¹²*Then the disciples approached and said to him, "Do you know that the Pharisees took offense when they heard what you said?"* ¹³*He answered, "Every plant that my heavenly Father has not planted will be*

uprooted. [14]*Let them alone; they are blind guides of the blind. And if one blind person guides another, both will fall into a pit."* [15]*But Peter said to him, "Explain this parable to us."* [16]*Then he said, "Are you also still without understanding?* [17]*Do you not see that whatever goes into the mouth enters the stomach, and goes out into the sewer?* [18]*But what comes out of the mouth proceeds from the heart, and this is what defiles.* [19]*For out of the heart come evil intentions, murder, adultery, fornication, theft, false witness, slander.* [20]*These are what defile a person, but to eat with unwashed hands does not defile."*

The clash between Jesus and the religious leaders developed into a controversy over the relative importance of "the tradition of the elders" (verse 2) and "the commandment of God" (verse 3). The tradition of the elders was a series of regulations and customs developed by the Pharisees to apply the Torah to everyday life, while the commandment of God was the teaching of the written law given by Moses. Taking an example of the Pharisaic tradition, the leaders ask why the disciples of Jesus do not wash their hands before eating. This practice did not develop as a matter of hygiene, but as a washing ritual to remove impurities for worship. Jesus responds by citing an example of the ways the Pharisees use their tradition to break a commandment of God. He says that their practice of pledging money and property to God excuses people from their obligation to materially support their aging parents with those funds. By contrasting the phrase "for God said" with "but you say," Jesus affirms that God's commandment to honor one's parents supersedes any pledge one has made to the temple (verses 4–5).

Since these issues of interpreting the Pharisaic traditions and the Torah were a matter of dispute within Judaism, Jesus offers a principle for discernment. What matters, he says, is what comes from the heart of a person, because what comes from the heart can either defile or bless. He chides his opponents with a quotation from Isaiah: "This people honors me with their lips, but their hearts are far from me" (verse 8). Jesus teaches that the food that goes into the mouth does not corrupt a person, but the evil that comes out of the mouth defiles, because "what comes out of the mouth proceeds from the heart" (verses 17–18). Purity of the heart is most fundamental for all religious practices.

These words of Jesus are an invitation to his listeners to open their hearts to him. In contrast to Jesus, who leads the blind to sight and faith, his opponents are blind guides (verse 14). With a vivid and memorable proverb, Jesus says, "If one blind person guides another, both will fall into a pit." Because their priorities are so distorted, the religious opponents of Jesus are leading themselves and others toward disaster and ruin. Jesus certainly does not set aside all Jewish practices; in fact, he demonstrates that his teachings are in accord with the Torah and the prophets. Rather, Jesus places purity of heart at the center, so that from the human heart united with God's will all religious practices flow.

Reflection and Discussion

• Sometimes we get so caught up in the doing we forget that the core issue for God is the state of our hearts. What words of Jesus particularly express this truth most clearly?

• What would be another example in which people sometimes honor God with their lips and not with their heart?

• For whom should I be a guide? What blindness must be healed in me so that my vision is clear enough to guide others?

Prayer

Lord, help me to honor you with my heart. Bring to light those things in my heart that need to change so that my words and actions may proceed from a heart devoted to doing your will.

He took the seven loaves and the fish; and after giving thanks he broke them and gave them to the disciples, and the disciples gave them to the crowds.

Matt 15:35–36

Jesus Continues to Heal and Feed Many

MATTHEW 15:21–39 *²¹Jesus left that place and went away to the district of Tyre and Sidon. ²²Just then a Canaanite woman from that region came out and started shouting, "Have mercy on me, Lord, Son of David; my daughter is tormented by a demon." ²³But he did not answer her at all. And his disciples came and urged him, saying, "Send her away, for she keeps shouting after us." ²⁴He answered, "I was sent only to the lost sheep of the house of Israel." ²⁵But she came and knelt before him, saying, "Lord, help me." ²⁶He answered, "It is not fair to take the children's food and throw it to the dogs." ²⁷She said, "Yes, Lord, yet even the dogs eat the crumbs that fall from their masters' table." ²⁸Then Jesus answered her, "Woman, great is your faith! Let it be done for you as you wish." And her daughter was healed instantly.*

²⁹After Jesus had left that place, he passed along the Sea of Galilee, and he went up the mountain, where he sat down. ³⁰Great crowds came to him, bringing with them the lame, the maimed, the blind, the mute, and many others. They put them at his feet, and he cured them, ³¹so that the crowd was amazed when they saw the mute speaking, the maimed whole, the lame walking, and the blind seeing. And they praised the God of Israel.

³²*Then Jesus called his disciples to him and said, "I have compassion for the crowd, because they have been with me now for three days and have nothing to eat; and I do not want to send them away hungry, for they might faint on the way." ³³The disciples said to him, "Where are we to get enough bread in the desert to feed so great a crowd?" ³⁴Jesus asked them, "How many loaves have you?" They said, "Seven, and a few small fish." ³⁵Then ordering the crowd to sit down on the ground, ³⁶he took the seven loaves and the fish; and after giving thanks he broke them and gave them to the disciples, and the disciples gave them to the crowds. ³⁷And all of them ate and were filled; and they took up the broken pieces left over, seven baskets full. ³⁸Those who had eaten were four thousand men, besides women and children. ³⁹After sending away the crowds, he got into the boat and went to the region of Magadan.*

Jesus has traversed the boundary separating the Jewish area of Galilee and the Gentile territory of Tyre and Sidon, crossing the barrier between bitter enemies, the Jews and their ancient rivals, the Canaanites. The Canaanite woman addresses Jesus three times. When she pleads for mercy upon herself and her demon-tormented daughter, Jesus responds with a silent rebuff. Apparently the woman continues to follow Jesus and his disciples, crying out behind them (verse 23). Annoyed by her behavior, the disciples urge Jesus to deal with her so that she will go away. Jesus then responds by stating his understanding of the divine mission he has embraced: "I was sent only to the lost sheep of the house of Israel" (verse 24). Jesus has an urgent sense of his mission to the people of Israel, and since the woman does not belong to the Jewish people, Jesus states that his mission is not for Gentiles.

Refusing to accept being ignored, the woman comes to the front side of the group and kneels before Jesus, effectively creating a roadblock in the way (verse 25). The woman is at the end of her rope, and, in one of the most moving gestures of the gospel, simply begs, "Lord, help me." She is absolutely confident that Jesus can heal her daughter if he is so inclined. But the response of Jesus seems shockingly heartless: "It is not fair to take the children's food and throw it to the dogs" (verse 26). His words, probably reflecting a common saying, compare Jews to the children of a family and Gentiles to scavenging dogs. Jesus cannot divert food to the Gentiles that is meant for the children of Israel, whom he has a mission to feed. Though some commentators suggest that

Jesus said these words with a playful twinkle in his eyes, it is difficult to imagine that these words would be anything less than insulting.

With relentless persistence, the woman then cleverly adapts the metaphor of Jesus' saying to her own situation: "Yes, Lord, yet even the dogs eat the crumbs that fall from their masters' table" (verse 27). In Greek culture, dogs were often the household pets and were present under the table during the family meals. The children would often share their food with the dogs. Surely the children of Israel, she thought, could share some of God's abundance with the Gentile dogs. She shifts Jesus' image of frugality, in which there is only enough food for the children, to an image of abundance, in which the food on the table is so plentiful that there is enough to feed the dogs beneath. By addressing him continuously as "Lord," she insists that he is Lord not only of Jews, but of Gentiles as well.

Jesus honors the woman for her charming wit and unshakable faith, and he instantly heals her daughter. By challenging anyone who would set boundaries and limits to those who would be called sons and daughters of God, this Canaanite women foreshadows the response of the Gentiles to the gospel in the early church. Jesus' granting of her request approves the woman's attitude and provides for the early church a warrant for its mission to the Gentiles by grounding that mission in the earthly ministry of Jesus himself.

This image of the abundant table feeding all of God's family is continued in the second feeding account (verses 32–38). Like the first feeding of the hungry crowds, this scene alludes to images of Moses feeding God's people in the desert and of the abundant banquet of God's kingdom. This time Jesus feeds the hungry crowds with seven loaves, and there are seven baskets full of leftovers. Because the number "seven" symbolizes abundance and completeness, the meal more clearly alludes to the plentiful food of God's kingdom. The Greek word for "giving thanks" is the source of the Christian term Eucharist, underscoring the connection to the eucharistic practices in the church to which Matthew wrote.

Reflection and Discussion

• Why would Jesus have ignored and then insulted the Canaanite woman? What is so admirable about her?

• In what ways does the Canaanite woman represent all the Gentiles? How does she move Jesus to envision his mission more inclusively?

• What are the main differences between the first and second feeding accounts? How does Jesus feeding the hungry crowds foreshadow the life of the early church?

Prayer

Lord Jesus, all people desire the nourishing food of your life. I thank you for feeding me with the bread of your kingdom. Help me to distribute the bread of life to the hungry people in the world around me.

You know how to interpret the appearance of the sky,
but you cannot interpret the signs of the times. Matt 16:3

The Leaven of the Pharisees and Sadducees

MATTHEW 16:1–12 ¹*The Pharisees and Sadducees came, and to test Jesus they asked him to show them a sign from heaven.* ²*He answered them, "When it is evening, you say, 'It will be fair weather, for the sky is red.'* ³*And in the morning, 'It will be stormy today, for the sky is red and threatening.' You know how to interpret the appearance of the sky, but you cannot interpret the signs of the times.* ⁴*An evil and adulterous generation asks for a sign, but no sign will be given to it except the sign of Jonah." Then he left them and went away.*

⁵*When the disciples reached the other side, they had forgotten to bring any bread.* ⁶*Jesus said to them, "Watch out, and beware of the yeast of the Pharisees and Sadducees."* ⁷*They said to one another, "It is because we have brought no bread."* ⁸*And becoming aware of it, Jesus said, "You of little faith, why are you talking about having no bread?* ⁹*Do you still not perceive? Do you not remember the five loaves for the five thousand, and how many baskets you gathered?* ¹⁰*Or the seven loaves for the four thousand, and how many baskets you gathered?* ¹¹*How could you fail to perceive that I was not speaking about bread? Beware of the yeast of the Pharisees and Sadducees!"* ¹²*Then they understood that he had not told them to beware of the yeast of bread, but of the teaching of the Pharisees and Sadducees.*

The opponents of Jesus continue to seek a "sign from heaven" (verse 1), some spectacular and undeniable indication of Jesus' power and authority. Jesus replies by noting how they use their folk knowledge to read signs in the sky that indicate the coming weather, but they are unable to see the indications of God's kingdom in the teachings and miracles of Jesus. The religious leaders do not question Jesus with sincerity, but like the devil in the wilderness, they seek to "test" Jesus. They already have plenty of signs, but they fail to respond with faith. They are oblivious to "the signs of the times," the indications that the hopes of Scripture are being fulfilled and that God's kingdom has come near (verses 3). Surely that is more important than the appearance of the sky, which indicates whether the weather will be stormy or clear. Jesus again offers them only "the sign of Jonah." Those who can read the signs of the times should realize that Jesus' call to repentance and his proclamation of God's kingdom are no less urgent than Jonah's message.

When Jesus again meets his disciples, he warns them to beware of "the yeast of the Pharisees and Sadducees" (verse 6). Thinking that Jesus was referring to material bread, the disciples fail to understand his meaning. Yeast is a substance that has an inner vitality; it has a pervading influence and transforming effect upon what it enters. In Jesus' parable of the yeast, the leaven mysteriously yet powerfully makes the whole batch of dough rise. The leavening influence of yeast can have a good or an evil influence. The leaven of the kingdom promotes the good; the leaven of the Pharisees and Sadducees, the influence of their sign-seeking skepticism, is a corrupting element that goes against the gospel message. Jesus leads his disciples to understand that the two miracles of the loaves were not only about leavened bread, but about the powerful leaven of the kingdom and its ability to feed the deepest hungers of God's people (verses 9–11). The disciples finally understand that Jesus is not speaking about mere bread. Rather, he is demonstrating the difference between trusting God for one's daily bread and anxious worry about the next meal.

While it is easy to criticize these religious leaders as they are presented in the gospel, we might ask ourselves if we fail in similar ways. There is a tendency in everyone to seek a "sign from heaven" rather than reading "the signs of the times." Rather than seeking after amazing and supernatural occurrences, Jesus challenges us to see God's work in the midst of the world in which we live. If we cannot understand that, then we are as obtuse as the disciples who confuse the kingdom-centered message of Jesus with their need for physical bread.

Reflection and Discussion

• In what way do the religious leaders express a tendency that is within each of us? What were they hoping to see in the sky?

• What are the teachings or religious views that disciples should be wary of today?

• Rather than looking to the sky, on what do I need to focus in order to see the signs of God's kingdom around me? What are some of the "signs of the times" today?

Prayer

Lord Jesus, open my eyes to see the signs of the kingdom in the midst of the world today. Help me to understand that you will provide for my daily bread while I focus my highest priority on being an instrument of your reign in the lives of others.

"You are Peter, and on this rock I will build my church, and the gates of Hades will not prevail against it." Matt 16:18

Peter Confesses that Jesus Is the Messiah

MATTHEW 16:13–28 [13]*Now when Jesus came into the district of Caesarea Philippi, he asked his disciples, "Who do people say that the Son of Man is?"* [14]*And they said, "Some say John the Baptist, but others Elijah, and still others Jeremiah or one of the prophets."* [15]*He said to them, "But who do you say that I am?"* [16]*Simon Peter answered, "You are the Messiah, the Son of the living God."* [17]*And Jesus answered him, "Blessed are you, Simon son of Jonah! For flesh and blood has not revealed this to you, but my Father in heaven.* [18]*And I tell you, you are Peter, and on this rock I will build my church, and the gates of Hades will not prevail against it.* [19]*I will give you the keys of the kingdom of heaven, and whatever you bind on earth will be bound in heaven, and whatever you loose on earth will be loosed in heaven."* [20]*Then he sternly ordered the disciples not to tell anyone that he was the Messiah.*

[21]*From that time on, Jesus began to show his disciples that he must go to Jerusalem and undergo great suffering at the hands of the elders and chief priests and scribes, and be killed, and on the third day be raised.* [22]*And Peter took him aside and began to rebuke him, saying, "God forbid it, Lord! This must never happen to you."* [23]*But he turned and said to Peter, "Get behind me, Satan! You are a stumbling block to me; for you are setting your mind not on divine things but on human things."*

²⁴Then Jesus told his disciples, "If any want to become my followers, let them deny themselves and take up their cross and follow me. ²⁵For those who want to save their life will lose it, and those who lose their life for my sake will find it. ²⁶For what will it profit them if they gain the whole world but forfeit their life? Or what will they give in return for their life?

²⁷"For the Son of Man is to come with his angels in the glory of his Father, and then he will repay everyone for what has been done. ²⁸Truly I tell you, there are some standing here who will not taste death before they see the Son of Man coming in his kingdom."

This crucial passage marks the major turning point of the gospel and propels the narrative of Jesus into its second half. Jesus has traveled with his disciples to the northernmost location in the gospel, the region of Caesarea Philippi. There is now a clear distance between his opponents and his closest disciples, on whom Jesus will focus for the remainder of the gospel. Matthew distinguishes between the communities of his opponents, which throughout the gospel are called "their synagogues," and the community of the Jewish followers of Jesus, which he calls the "church" (*ekklesia* in Greek; verse 18).

The first half of the gospel has led to the question that Jesus asks of his disciples: "Who do you say that I am?" (verse 15). Everyone who encounters the person of Jesus through the ages must respond to this central question. Simon Peter's response, "You are the Messiah, the Son of the living God," expresses a faith that is not possible through superior human insight, but only through God's grace (verse 17). Because Peter has spoken not through human experience but rather through divine revelation, Jesus declares him uniquely blessed.

Now that Simon Peter has announced who Jesus is, Jesus declares who Peter is. Jesus gives Simon the new name "Peter," which, in effect, bestows upon him a new identity. In the language of the gospel, the Greek name Petros creates a wordplay with *petra*, the Greek word for rock. In Aramaic, the language of Jesus and his earliest followers, the saying is even more exact: "You are *kepha*, and on this *kepha* I will build my church" (verse 18). The parallelism makes it clear that Peter himself is the rock, the sturdy foundation upon which Jesus will construct his church. Jesus has already declared that any wise builder constructs his house on rock (7:24–25). With such a solid base, the house will not fall despite the fiercest of storms. Now Jesus announces that he will build his church on the foundation of Peter, "and the gates of Hades will not prevail against it." These gates of the netherworld represent the powers of death and evil. With such a firm foundation, the church will not crumble or fall despite the fiercest of opposition.

When Jesus hands Peter "the keys of the kingdom" (verse 19), he is offering him the means of opening the way to life for countless people. The church is not the kingdom, but it is the imperfect earthly agent of God's kingdom. Through Peter's preaching and leadership within the church, he will lead people into God's kingdom. A similar image occurs in Isaiah where a certain Eliakim is made "master of the household" and given "the key of the house of David" with the authority to open and shut the gates for those seeking entry into the palace (Isa 22:22). As keeper of the keys, Peter is made the master of Jesus' household, with the privilege of welcoming people into the church. The authority to "bind" and "loose" can refer to admitting or excluding people, imposing rules and sanctions, or interpreting and applying the teachings of Jesus for the church.

From this point in the gospel, Jesus turns from teaching and healing the crowds and begins to teach his disciples the meaning of his life. Jesus explains that it is not his mission to be a powerful, conquering Messiah or a glorious, regal Son of God. His prediction of his suffering, death, and resurrection summarizes the entire second half of the gospel (verse 21). There is no other way than the way of the cross, the inevitable result of his whole life of self-giving and love. But this is too much for the impulsive Peter, and he takes Jesus aside to argue with him. How could the long-awaited king, the great hope of Israel, come to such a disgraceful end? Peter's response, "God forbid it, Lord! This must never happen to you," shows how far Peter is at this point from understanding the implications of Jesus' mission (verse 22).

Jesus' response to Peter contains some of the harshest words recorded from Jesus' mouth (verse 23). He calls Peter a "Satan," a tempter. Peter is trying to deflect Jesus from the path that God had set before him. Peter is tempting Jesus to take the easy way out, to give in to selfish desires for security and glory. Jesus replies, calling Peter an obstacle, "a stumbling block," in his path. The rock of the church has become an obstruction, like a big rock in the way of Jesus' mission. Yet, Jesus does not tell Peter, "Away with you, Satan," as he had told his tempter in the wilderness (4:10); rather, Jesus tells Peter, "Get behind me, Satan," commanding him to resume his position as a follower, walking behind Jesus in discipleship.

Despite the spotlight that shines on the figure of Peter throughout the gospel, Matthew refuses to idealize him. He highlights his weakness and failures along with his sturdy faith and pre-eminent role among the disciples. Before Peter could truly follow Jesus, he had to learn the cost of discipleship: "If any want to become my followers, let them deny themselves and take up their cross and follow me" (verse 24). Peter had to learn from Jesus how to replace his self-centered ambition and desire for prestige with recognition of the value of self-sacrifice. He had to learn how to lose himself in Christ, to take up his mission, his way of life, and his very identity as his own. Peter had to learn that being a disciple of Jesus means taking up the cross, not grudgingly enduring it but embracing it, being willing to suffer for the gospel, and getting behind Jesus in order to follow in the way that he leads.

Reflection and Discussion

• In what sense does Peter's mindset become momentarily satanic? How is Peter's way of thinking a danger to all disciples?

• Jesus teaches his disciples the message of denial before the feast, suffering before the glory, service before the reign, cross before the crown. What do these truths express to me about the nature of God's kingdom in the world?

• What is the significance of giving Simon a new name with his new role? How does the symbol of the keys express this role?

• How did Peter the rock become a stumbling block? What is the lesson here for my discipleship and for the church?

• What has Matthew's gospel taught me thus far about being a disciple of Jesus?

Prayer

Messiah and Son of God, you built your church on the foundation of Peter and the apostles, and you welcome people into the community of faith in every age. Deepen my faith in you and help me to carry out the mission you have given me in your church.

SUGGESTIONS FOR FACILITATORS, GROUP SESSION 6

1. Welcome group members and make any final announcements or requests.

2. You may want to pray this prayer as a group:

Eternal King, you gave your Son to be our teacher and model for living in your kingdom. Be with us as we develop our discipleship and face the challenges of following in the way of Jesus. Assure us that you understand our needs and provide for our daily bread when we place our trust in you. Continue to form our hearts so that we will be devoted to doing your will without fear and serving those in need with generosity. May we work together to build your church on earth and welcome others into the life of your kingdom.

3. Ask one or more of the following questions:
   - How has this study of Matthew's gospel enriched your life?
   - In what way has this study challenged you the most?

4. Discuss lessons 25 through 30. Choose one or more of the questions for reflection and discussion from each lesson to discuss as a group.

5. Ask the group if they would like to study another in the Threshold Bible Study series. Discuss the topic and dates, and make a decision among those interested. Ask the group members to suggest people they would like to invite to participate in the next study series.

6. Ask the group to discuss the insights that stand out most from this study over the past six weeks.

7. Conclude by praying aloud the following prayer or another of your own choosing:

Holy Spirit of the living God, you inspired the writers of the Scriptures and you have guided our study during these weeks. Continue to deepen our love for the word of God in the holy Scriptures and draw us more deeply into the heart of Jesus. We thank you for the confident hope you have placed within us, and for the gifts that build up the church. Through this study, lead us to worship and witness more fully and fervently, and bless us now and always with the fire of your love.

THE **GOSPEL OF MATTHEW** IN THE SUNDAY LECTIONARY

KEY: **Reading** Sunday or feast *(Lectionary #-Cycle)*

Matthew 1:1–25
Christmas: Vigil Mass
(13-ABC)

Matthew 1:18–24
4th Sunday of Advent *(10-A)*

Matthew 2:1–12
The Epiphany of the Lord
(20-ABC)

Matthew 2:13–15, 19–23
Sunday in Octave of
Christmas: Holy Family *(17-A)*

Matthew 3:1–12
2nd Sunday of Advent *(4-A)*

Matthew 3:13–17
Sunday after Epiphany:
Baptism of the Lord *(21-A)*

Matthew 4:1–11
1st Sunday of Lent *(22-A)*

Matthew 4:12–23
3rd Sunday in OT *(67-A)*

Matthew 5:1–12a
4th Sunday in OT *(70-A)*

Matthew 5:13–16
5th Sunday in OT *(73-A)*

Matthew 5:17–37
6th Sunday in OT *(76-A)*

Matthew 5:38–48
7th Sunday in OT *(79-A)*

Matthew 6:24–34
8th Sunday in OT *(82-A)*

Matthew 7:21–27
9th Sunday in OT *(85-A)*

Matthew 9:9–13
10th Sunday in OT *(88-A)*

Matthew 9:36—10:8
11th Sunday in OT *(91-A)*

Matthew 10:26–33
12th Sunday in OT *(94-A)*

Matthew 10:37–42
13th Sunday in OT *(97-A)*

Matthew 11:2–11
3rd Sunday of Advent *(7-A)*

Matthew 11:25–30
14th Sunday in OT *(100-A)*

Matthew 13:1–23
15th Sunday in OT *(103-A)*

Matthew 13:24–43
16th Sunday in OT *(106-A)*

Matthew 13:44–52
17th Sunday in OT *(109-A)*

Matthew 14:13–21
18th Sunday in OT *(112-A)*

Matthew 14:22–33
19th Sunday in OT *(115-A)*

Matthew 15:21–28
20th Sunday in OT *(118-A)*

Matthew 16:13–20
21st Sunday in OT *(121-A)*

Matthew 16:21–27
22nd Sunday in OT *(124-A)*

Matthew 17:1–9
2nd Sunday of Lent *(25-A)*

Matthew 18:15–20
23rd Sunday in OT *(127-A)*

Matthew 18:21–35
24th Sunday in OT *(130-A)*

Matthew 20:1–16a
25th Sunday in OT *(133-A)*

Matthew 21:1–11
Palm Sunday:
Procession of Palms *(37-A)*

Matthew 21:28–32
26th Sunday in OT *(136-A)*

Matthew 21:33–43
27th Sunday in OT *(139-A)*

Matthew 22:1–14
28th Sunday in OT *(142-A)*

Matthew 22:15–21
29th Sunday in OT *(145-A)*

Matthew 22:34–40
30th Sunday in OT *(148-A)*

Matthew 23:1–12
31st Sunday in OT *(151-A)*

Matthew 24:37–44
1st Sunday of Advent *(1-A)*

Matthew 25:1–13
32nd Sunday in OT *(154-A)*

Matthew 25:14–30
33rd Sunday in OT *(157-A)*

Matthew 25:31–46
34th Sunday in OT:
Christ the King *(160-A)*

Matthew 26:14—27:66
Palm Sunday of the
Lord's Passion *(38-A)*

Matthew 28:1–10
Easter Vigil *(41-A)*

Matthew 28:16–20
Ascension of the Lord *(58-A)*

Matthew 28:16–20
Sunday after Pentecost:
Holy Trinity (165-B)

ORDERING ADDITIONAL STUDIES

AVAILABLE TITLES IN THIS SERIES INCLUDE...

Advent Light

Angels of God

Divine Mercy

Eucharist

The Feasts of Judaism

The Holy Spirit
and Spiritual Gifts

Jerusalem, the Holy City

The Lamb and the Beasts

Mysteries of the Rosary

The Names of Jesus

People of the Passion

Pilgrimage in the Footsteps
of Jesus

The Resurrection and the Life

The Sacred Heart of Jesus

Stewardship of the Earth

The Tragic and Triumphant Cross

Jesus, the Messianic King
(PART 1): MATTHEW 1–16

Jesus, the Messianic King
(PART 2): MATTHEW 17–28

Jesus, the Word Made Flesh
(PART 1): JOHN 1–10

Jesus, the Word Made Flesh
(PART 2): JOHN 11–21

Jesus, the Suffering Servant
(PART 1): MARK 1–8

Jesus, the Suffering Servant
(PART 2): MARK 9–16

Jesus, the Compassionate
Savior (PART 1): LUKE 1–11

Jesus, the Compassionate
Savior (PART 2): LUKE 12–24

Church of the Holy Spirit
(PART 1): ACTS OF THE APOSTLES 1-14

Church of the Holy Spirit
(PART 2): ACTS OF THE APOSTLES 15-28

FOR MORE INFORMATION, VISIT OUR WEBSITE
WWW.23RDPUBLICATIONS.COM OR CALL US AT **1-800-321-0411**

TWENTY-THIRD PUBLICATIONS